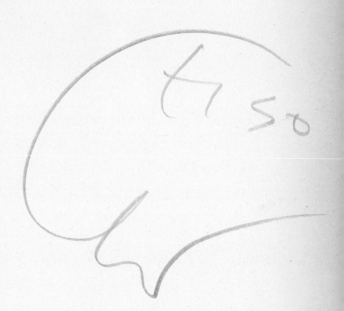

Poems 1978–1985

EDWARD BOND was born and educated in London. His first play, *The Pope's Wedding*, was staged at the Royal Court Theatre in 1962, where it was followed by *Saved* in 1965, *Early Morning* in 1968, *Lear* in 1971, *The Sea* in 1973, *Bingo* in 1974, *The Fool* in 1975 and *Restoration* in 1981. *The Bundle* (1978) and his trilogy, *The War Plays* (1985), were staged by the Royal Shakespeare Company, and *The Woman* (1978) and *Summer* (1982) were both at the National Theatre. *We Come to the River*, an opera by Henze to a libretto by Bond, was premièred at Covent Garden in 1976. He has written a number of shorter plays mostly for fringe theatres as well as translations and adaptations of plays by Chekhov, Wedekind and Webster. His first book of poetry, *Theatre Poems and Songs*, was published in 1978.

The photograph of Edward Bond on the back cover is by Charles N. White.

by the same author

The Pope's Wedding
Saved
Early Morning
Narrow Road to the Deep North
Lear
The Sea
Bingo
The Fool & We Come to the River
A-A-America! & Stone
The Bundle
The Woman
The Worlds with The Activists Papers
Restoration & The Cat
Summer
Derek & Choruses from After The Assassinations
Human Cannon
The War Plays: A Trilogy

in the World Dramatists series

Plays: One (The Pope's Wedding, Saved, Early Morning)
Plays: Two (Lear, The Sea, Narrow Road to the Deep North,
Black Mass *and* Passion)
Plays: Three (Bingo, The Fool, The Woman, Stone)
also available

Theatre Poems and Songs
Spring Awakening by Frank Wedekind
(translated by Edward Bond)

Edward Bond

Poems 1978–1985

A Methuen Paperback

A Methuen Paperback

First published as an original paperback in 1987 in Great Britain
by Methuen London Ltd, 11 New Fetter Lane, London EC4P 4EE
and in the United States of America by Methuen Inc,
29 West 35th Street, New York, NY10001.
Copyright © 1987 by Edward Bond

Printed and bound in Great Britain by
Redwood Burn Limited, Trowbridge, Wiltshire

British Library Cataloguing in Publication Data

Bond, Edward
Poems, 1978–1985.
I. Title
821'.914   PR6052.05

ISBN 0 413 16500 0

Contents

Introduction

A few of these poems were written for programmes for productions of my plays. But by far most were scribbled on scraps of paper, or bills, cartons, the backs of letters and so on, and left around to accumulate. In boasting of their humble origin I pay my respects to the first principle of art.

They were written in roughly the order they have in this book. Some were written as cycles (these are obvious) and I have arranged the others into sections. Some of the sections are named after their poems' origins – for example the poems in 'The Rothbury Guidebook' were written at Rothbury and those in 'Going to Work' were written in the train as I went to rehearse *The War Plays*. Other sections are named after the form of their poems – for example the 'Elegies' and 'Songs'.

The 'Sonnets' are not in usual sonnet form. When I reread the poems some of them reminded me of the concentrated way in which sonnets state, elaborate and resolve – or evade – their themes. This precedent (though I hope not the evasion) must have been in my mind when I wrote these poems so I've now called them sonnets. I should add that the 'Elegies', 'Discourses' and so on did not originally have these names.

The book does not contain poems and songs from plays or which have already been published with plays.

My publisher has asked me to account for the punctuation. My punctuation is . . . mine. A poem has its own 'feeling' and the punctuation and the use of capitals should accord with this feeling. I punctuate on moral principles, so you can hardly expect consistency.

When I reworked and arranged the poems I found myself creating dramatic structures for the book and each of its sections. I had not written the poems for a book but I'm sure that without noticing it I'd been using my habit of working with larger dramatic structures to isolate and define these briefer experiences. So the poems 'make' a book.

The 'Work Poems' are in part to do with the people and events of my recent plays. Perhaps they can't be understood unless these plays are known. I don't think so and in any case they are few. I think they are part of the book's structure and lead to its last section. This section concerns nuclear holocaust. Nuclear holocaust is for our time the only subject – directly or by reflection – for art. Art engages (within the artist's limitations) its spectators in such a way that they wish – or (frankly) are forced – to recreate themselves in experiencing it: they can only experience it by judging it. Whenever we pass a judgement we judge ourself. The standards by which we judge art are those by which we live. Art either liberates or imperils. Like bombs or food, it goes to the core of our lives. We cannot escape its consequences and they may be more far-reaching than those of bombs and food. Bad food poisons those who eat it; bad art is a famine passed on to the unborn. Bombs destroy cities; bad art gives life to the bombmakers' culture, which persuades them they have a political need and a moral right to make bombs.

Daniel Baron Cohen, David Hirst, Philip Roberts and Katharine Worth read a draft of the book. I am grateful for their suggestions and included all of them when I revised the poems. In this way I paid my respects to the second principle of art: to see the world through other people's eyes.

Then who is to blame or praise for what we see? The poems offer an answer.

E.B.

The
Rothbury
Guidebook

The Rothbury Guidebook

When the War was Over

The survivors didnt look in their children's faces

You gave us life
You gave us the right
To ask you to die for us
To spare us your shame

So the survivors led their children over the graves
Into the ruins
And began to live again

Patience

From our windows we watch
Those we have loved chased and beaten
And if our enemies took away the sky
We would keep our flags
As if there was still somewhere to fly them
If they denied us land for our graves
We would still strive to bear
The miseries they heap on us
Though these miseries are killing
So patient are we

From the North Hill

From the north hill
The dark slate roofs
Like iron ploughshares
November mist
Late afternoon

A flock of racing pigeons
Rises and swings from side to side
Backward and forwards
At each turn flashing
From grey to white or white to grey
As if a flag waved
Over the town

How We See

After Treblinka
And the spezialkommando
Who tore a child with bare hands
Before its mother in Warsaw
We see differently

Men taken from workshops and farms to fight for kaiser and
    king
Lived in a world asleep in mist
The spezialkommando lived in a world of electric lights
    cinemas planes and radios
We see racist slogans chalked on walls differently
We see walls differently

Crocuses and Coltsfoot

Yesterday snow fell
This morning it lies grey under sleet
And the mauve crocuses
And yellow coltsfoot
Do not stand in the pride of spring
But of men on pavements
Arrested and going to die

The Rothbury Guidebook

Down from the Callay Crag there is a small upright rock with
a hollowed-out room said to have once been the home of a
hermit. This rock may be hard to find.

Rothbury and District Guide

In the forest clearing there is a stone
In which is cut a room
Where sages live
And from the town come women
With children on their shoulders
And factory men
Singing and dressed in robes
That flap in the wind
Families sit on the grass to eat
The lovers' limbs grow from each other's body
Children peep into the hollow
At the crumpled rug and blankets
And young and old talk with the sages
And at night I dreamed that on the rock
A turret and battlements had been built
And every beast had a hunter
And every tree an axe

The rock may be hard to find

Tanks

In the night wind roared in the garden
I heard tanks going to battle
The jubilation of the crowd before the leader

In the morning I found
Two trees on the lawn
With shattered trunks

On Hearing Singing from a University Church

From this century we have planes to fly between cities
We have rid ourselves of many diseases
We do not work like beasts
The harvests are rich
Hunger no longer drives our poor to eat orange peel they
    pick up in the street
Yet it is also the century of wars and the gassing of races
In asia and africa the poor starve
Weapons ? – more than savages !
And a soldier has walked on the moon

There have been revolutions in which we may hope
But here the texts of change are kept in libraries
Christian relics: the doctrine that we are animals to be
    haltered – a god who slew his son – songs in the juju house
The twenty-seven crystal spheres are broken but we turn in
    constellations of mud
When will we have the ideas of this century ?

The greeks said know yourself
When will we know where the street on which we live leads ?
Who works for whom in our factories ?
Who eats from our plate ? Who thinks with our head ?
When will we stop making debris for children to play with ?
When will we have the ideas of this century ?

Grove

Doldona's ancient grove where there is always sighing
Of pines in wind
Of distant sounds from the village
Voices – the milk lorry – a barking dog

Grey trunks as long as masts lie on dead needles
Rocks jut like prows of sunken ships
A scattered flock of startled sheep runs together
Then rolls down the hill below
Like a cloth blown from a table

Under the mountain the river lies on the valley floor
A chainmail corslet hacked into strips
And thrown down from a cavalryman's body
As he leaned on a rock

Life cost pain and early death
And laughter at things we no longer laugh at
But the old beliefs and illusions
Are like the wind in these fallen trees
And this year's grass

Montrose

I walk on the shore
Long nets ten feet high
Line after line after line
Stretch from below high tide
To the sea

When the tide rises
Water covers the nets
When it falls
Fish swim along the nets
Till the snares at the ends
Are full of fish

The fish below held flat
By fish flailing on top
Cannot move in their pain
And are still and silent and drown

In the bright sun and sharp wind
The wooden stakes and cords
Sparkle with frost-white salt

After an hour
I start to walk back beside my footsteps
Soon they are blurred
The wind fills them with sand
Long before I reach the place where I started
They have gone
As if I had not been there

Abandoned Factory

Grey bricks
The classical façade of a country mansion
And over the main door red bricks set in the curve of a
    norman arch
A home for machines
Broken glass in stone mullions
Sheets from american mags on the stone stairs
In the floors where the looms were bolted – holes

Workers spent their working life here
First came at ten
Worked twelve hours a day for six days
Laughed in corners
Courted and married and bore children
And later left or died
In the methodist churchyard there are eight generations
The children lying on top of their parents

What trace of them is left in the house of machines ?
No stone scrolls on the walls or memorial trees in the yard
So many years and only holes in the floors ?
And then I saw between the holes
Stones worn down by feet

After Talking to a Meeting of University Students

Many studied into the small hours
Their long factory shifts were like shadows in the room
The first time they bought a book a new guilt disturbed them
Money should be spent on things to be worn or eaten
Strange temptation ! – to buy something that grows when
    consumed !

Now before me rows of faces like books on shelves
Here wisdom can grow in daylight !
So I asked what wisdom was
But all they had got from books was dust and worms
They told me life was absurd
Death is a runner who comes from behind
His shadow trips you and he strikes
We are beasts fed by the butcher

In africa – it was filmed – an infant in its dead mother's arms
     stirs in the last sleep of famine
In england a factory worker trembles with palsy at thirty
In asia a drunken driver runs down a girl
In america a mother dies of cancer: in the street a south seas
     paradise on a cigarette hoarding ad
In ireland a dead boy in a gutter: the army hands round a
     beer can
In italy a grandfather murdered for a few lire: a youth in
     jeans stands before a judge in a medieval jester's cap

We are not beasts who pass a few days tied to a butcher's
     cart
We speak of truth and bury our dead with as much care as if
     they were the living
Each death is as different as each life
It comes towards us and many run to meet it
Its bones rattle like the coins for which the living are sold

The world is not absurd
Our lives are absurd
Our cities and towns are absurd
And study is absurd and turns us into fools
Unless it teaches us to change our cities and towns and the
     way we live

Hilltop

I reached the hilltop
And looked down the steep stone cliff
To the lake eight hundred feet below
And saw close to an invasion of reeds
Three white shapes under water
Large even from where I stood
And as I thought of wars and sheets on the dead
Slowly the white shapes rose to the surface
And three swans unfolded
Not shaking away water they calmly floated across the lake

The Plain

Looking down from the high mountain
I see the caravan trekking over the plain
The elders drive the waggons
The children shout in wonder
At night food is cooked over the camp fires
And the horses graze on short hobbles
I would like to be a rock to shelter them from the wind
A cliff to shield them from their enemies
A forest to keep them from the rain
A black leopard to appear before them in the pass
They would chase me with their guns and I would lead them
    to the waterhole
But when I go down to the plain I hear the leopard's laugh
    in the children's shout
And as the elders ask me to sit I see in their faces and the
    hands that serve the meal
The cliffs in the mountains

Clouds

Dust clouds coiling high as smoke from a volcano
Raised by an army of people marching over a plain
And on the clouds flicker images of cattle and fields
Houses factories bridges and boats
Towers and trees and children playing at women's feet
And fathers with children on their backs
As if they carried parcels to houses not yet built
Flickering and fading and flashing
On the whirling clouds above the army
That marches over the plain and carries the world on its
    back

Chaffinch

When in the city I see
A flock of flying birds
I count
Nine ten . . . twenty
Here I see claws as thin as hairs
The unblinking eyes in the bush of feathers
And how the snow holds out the walking chaffinch's wings
As if it were a toy
Carved from wood and painted

You Wake Me

Bright chaffinch as painted as a clown
Foraging for seeds in snow
In spring flying through the garden
With a beakful of rubble to build
In summer feeding the mouths
In your oracle tree
In autumn on a wall away from the wind
With feathers ruffled
Each morning you wake in silence
And then wake me

A Gift

Turning on the edge of the sea
Red seaweed or a rotting fish ?
As the waves go back
It snags on a rock
A scarf !

I hold it high to dry in the wind
Then knot it on my neck

Walk

The black line of rivulet on the snow-buried hill
Comes down to the rock and falls
Grey and white
To the granite pool below

Light snow that first touched the earth this morning
Now roars on the dark granite and silent stones
High in the air crows drift like smuts from fires
And these black trees at the roadside
Are as simple as the ground that guards the unborn spring

I walk down the hill
At peace in a world of disaster
From the chimneys a smoke haze drifts
Like breath on a winter morning

Sledging

After the race down
With a head full of speed
The slow climb up
Slipping in snow
Dragging the heavy sledge
At last time to think
The plodding feet seem to enjoy it

Mating Dogs

Two dogs on the snow-covered lawn
The hound struts briskly in circles round the bitch
She casually forages for scents
Their black eyes and the little black tips of their ears and
    tails
Jiggle – then he mounts in the very centre
Of the lawn
With what modesty the white dogs came to this white place !
And the lewd city-dogs
    They do it on street corners to protect their masters' eyes

Midnight

Midnight
I open the door for the dog
The church clock
Strikes the time in the graveyard
The music is stately
I stand still
An owl in the dark garden
Passes close to me before the stars
I return to my desk
Even a churchtower
May be useful

Scare

Half-way through the night
I wake afraid
The roar of an avalanche !
It is the snow
Falling from the roof
The thaw has set in

Wind

Wind blows the white clouds
Over the bright blue sky
I stand on the green lawn
And unwrap my linen shirt
To look at my worm-white body
Or worse – the bier
On which winter lay
And in the cold wind
My skin puckers and shivers
With life

Aspen

On the thin arms of the aspen
By the river – buds
Happier I walk on
It grows straight
I was in the world before it
When I am dead others will see
Green buds on it
And other trees

Larches

Fool I was always here !
I merely slept
And covered my breast with my hands
Now I have taken my hands away

Shouldnt I sleep ?
I worked in spring and harvest
Kept the fire to cook at by day
And at night held a lamp over your head
Now look ! my firstborn
The bright leaves of the larches

River Hedge

Along the river a hedge
Full with bright new leaves
From the lower branches hang sticks and grass and trash
Left by the high river spate after the winter storms
A fringe bleached white by sun and wind

Children are born wise in this paradise !
They wear beards

Four Birches

On the top of the green hill four slender birches
Silver branches trembling
And in the blue sky thin clouds
Veils blown from brides

Ancient idols stand in cities that fell before our language was
    spoken
And rags flutter on sticks: war-totems less than skeletons that
    grin after victory
Dead soldiers' wounds staunched with gun-cotton ! Bound
    with flags !

But the raised arms of the four village birches are not locked
    in prayer
And the villagers pass through their shadows on the snow
    pushed open by the sun

Snow Letters

All afternoon I climbed into the moorland hills
Till time and space and light
Joined in a new world
The hares still wore white winter coats
Primroses grew by steep streams
Where they were easy to wash away
Curlews called like travellers lost at evening
And on the dark distant hills
The last snow lay in chinese letters – a huge white bird
Holding the hill in outstretched wings

Bent Trees

After a day of warm wind
Outside my window the trees bend
They answer my angry question
'We nod with the wisdom of age'
I relent
When they are down
(The axe leans in the shed doorway)
Sticks will be cut from their branches
So that even the old may walk upright

Industrial City

1.
In the black canal
Factory-crates prams and gas cookers
And three white swans floating
As the moon rises
On nights of terror

2.
In the industrial water reflections of passers-by
Smoke hovering over tall chimneys
As he goes home from the factory
The footsteps of the worker in the donkey-jacket
Sound in the silence on the stones of the towpath
Like the footsteps of the thinker
In the cloister

3.
The hill of small terraced houses rises
Above the canal and railway and churches
Anglican methodist RC and mad
And the town hall temple and castellated brick barracks
And as the train passes
The setting sun strikes every window and spire and roof
So that the hill blazes with fire

4.
On platforms and bridges and streets
Men and women with shopping bags and dusty shoes
And work in their shoulders
And friendly children pulling like guides at their hands
Pass with a hidden purpose in the city

Five Bridges

Early morning
I drew the curtains of the big window
In my room in the tower on the hill over Newcastle
Below me the river of five bridges
The ports and warehouses
Ships masts radar and gulls
Flats shops merchant-offices monuments
Motorways junctions churches and factories
The tiles glass concrete
Elizabethan daub and georgian brick
And saw a white ambulance enter the small victorian
    township of workers' houses at the foot of the hill
It urgently sought one house
But the search needed fantasy
So it wandered gaily from street to street
Till suddenly it found the street and shot in a straight line
The doors already opening like the wings of a landing swan
And stopped at the narrow curb by a door
Three minutes later the stretcher was carried out to the
    ambulance
The scarlet blanket as bright as a ruby ring on the narrow
    grey street
Actors should work with this fantasy
When they urgently search for the truth
And when they have found it
Startle the audience
With the speed and precision of their attack

After A Time Apart

After a time apart
I do not ask how to lie with her
Which cannot be unlearned
But how to lie at her side
And in the afternoon after the night
I lay beside her
Head to head and feet to feet
Then shoved it up
Plastering her inside with hairs
And in this crudity
Found gentleness

Morning

After love we lie in the early morning
Gentle wind in the leaves
Under the roof a sparrow shrieks
At the great wrongs of the world
My body swells as the sun rises
Over the edge of the hill
To see that all things are at peace

You lie still
An animal curled on my chest
Your hair on my shoulder
Breathing in whispers
Cool air runs in my nostrils
Like water over stones
So that I almost faint as I wake

Sheets

It is night and there will be no love
In darkness I carry the day's burden
You are with me
I hold you to touch your sleep
So that I sleep

And in the morning
When light stretches on the horizon
The earth raises her arms to lift the sun
As a mother holds her child to the window
And we are dazzled in our sheets

When the Right Took Power in England

The right took power in england
On the third day of may
It was bitterly cold on the third day of may
It snowed
And the cold set in

Violet

In its crumbled bloom
In the winter grass
A violet
One morning the child's dress in the bombed-out rubble
We see what the poets did not see
And do what the heroes and heroines left undone

Light

When the house is dark
When the sky is dark
When the day is dark
When the times are dark
When in darkness the river beats at the rock
When dark winds bend the trees to the ground
When we stumble in darkness
When we crouch in darkness
We will make a light
The world is in darkness because we have made a shadow
The sun seeks light
We will bring it back
And so in the time of darkness
Make light
In the dark house and in the sky

The Struggle

Looking back from the halfway
On a time of wars and well-run death camps
When a bomb to destroy the world was made
And men more dangerous than any who lived before
Walked freely in our streets
And that I have wasted some of my time
Neglected those in my care
And sometimes asked for help that was not given
Now that I know the things I can never do
And what my life's work is
And where the road leads though not if I shall get there
I am surprised to find no bitterness in me
I have accepted the struggle
These days I smile more

Missing Button

Let me be buried in jeans
And a white shirt
With bare feet
And from the neck of the shirt
A button missing
So that if at a later time
Men dig up our cities
They find not only bones
In rotting medals and braid
But I wait to greet them and tell
How in our time too
We were able to love
The things that are simple

Keep Going

It's a dead time
Things'll grow from this rain
But now there's mud
How often they've made mud and not built !
Find your footing
You're not clean ? Dont worry
No one's clean here !
It's hard to stand ?
Crawl !
Keep going in the time between winter and spring !

Nothing Else Matters

Last night in Wallsend
The young people spoke with accents so thick
I could not understand some of the lines I'd written
Yet the play had more to tell its audience
Than it had on the great city stages
They would have found the lies
If I had not written truths they proved every day of their life
So that they told my truth with their strength
And out in the cold I said
Write for them – nothing else matters
But those whose lives create truth
Should also speak
On the great city stages

The Table

The four windows of this stone house face west
My long table stands before one in the living-room
On it lie plays and poems
A dictionary and a guide to mammals
Envelopes and paper clips
A bowl of white narcissi
And a bowl of crocuses not yet open
What colour will they be ?
The notebook bound in black
From which this sheet was taken
Looks as solemn as the bible
But the metal clasps in the spine are open
And the sheets may be taken out to be used
And lately I have eaten at this table
Two times each day I clear a place for the plate
The glass and knife and fork
To eat among the books and watch through the window
Birds forage in the garden
The typewriter keys
The crumbs and sketches for work
Bring me peace
Soldiers may well feel this
When they sit on the grass outside their tent before battle

The Blanket

One winter in ancient china
A poet wished for a blanket so big
It covered a village
We honour the age of the buffalo
And the wooden plough
But ask for a roof
To shelter the world

Street Poem

Street Poem

Dorset Haiku

Gun Cliff Lyme Regis
Evening haze
At the left three cliffs
Staring to sea
Time held down in claws
Great waves have the shapes of little ones

Gull
Quay steps
Gull watches and eats
Dead prey jerks in claws
Next gull stalks it

Pear
Leaves soft gentle
Wind blows them back
I see the arms were always lifted in fright

Yew
The great yew bears the seasons well
At winter I touch the bark –
The green nails it grows for its crucifixion

Cedar
Grey branches heavy as tree-trunks hang to the ground
Skeleton of a vortex

Oak
Afternoon heavy with prey and sun
Lion stretched on a branch
Gazes at sea
Mask – white whiskers brittle as fishbone
Time to time the tail flickers
Deep inside the body

Elizabethan Portraits at Montecute
Black pupils stared
At heretical tracts
At lips under greybeards
At arraigned (smiled like pincers)
As they searched for the worm in the orchard
As they built warships and serenaded sundials
As they walked over bowling greens to the block: the living
    among a dead tableau
At the stairs as the servants left for the night
Eyes of dead whales on the seafloor

Latch
Back adder-dazzle
Rock wears stomach smooth – pale as blindman's eyelids
It crosses punctures and crevices
Suddenly appearing
Silent
Snake
In entrances against light

Mare
Hooves stamping water
Mane waves of a hundred seas
Spume on pink nostrils
Spray-dashed eyes
Tail thrashes foam
Whinnies after stallion
Kicking with pistols
At the shouting sea

Peach-faced Lovebirds

From India
Faces of blush pink
Grotesque as clown-masks

One knew a hole I couldnt find
At night it flew from the cage
Each morning it strutted on the wire roof
Screaming for food

Each day I caught it
And carefully carried it back
Its beak sharp and hooked

Till the morning I knocked it
With the net-frame
And it died

For days its mate called for its morning return
Then sat silent on a perch

Last night she found the hole
Went screaming along the hawthorn hedge after her dead
    lover
A bright bird in the grey fields

The cage is empty
My clown's hands lift the latch

Cranes at Tuft Bay

At first I didnt see the two specks
The cranes had changed shape and colour
Why do they fly so high over the curved shore
With the brown cliffs and orange gorse ?

If I could fly with those pale ghosts
Chests deep and strong as prows
Feathers sharp as arrow flights
Voices raucous as drunken sailors
With the deep blue stretched over me
And below the shore as white as hail
That's how Leonardo saw Monboso

From the cliff I see
Far out in the bay beyond reach of sound
Men throw nets from a boat

The sun sinks
In the mist the boat drifts over its own path

Daffodils in the Sick-room

I lie in the white sheets
Yellow horses in green harness come
Bowed but dragging nothing
To stand in a circle in the smithy's stream
Waiting to be shod

Distant mountains erase the words the fetlocks make in
    water
Horses do not ask what they carry but only the weight
They do not turn their heads when invisible fish
Tug at the kite in the river
It jerks as if in the wind

The fishermen's net is laid to dry on the bank
When gathered and cast it falls like the ghost of grass
     through the water
When hauled in full – the shape of things trying to get out
What is art ?
A ton of silk for the kitemaker ?
Ten thousand rivers in the land ?
Little waves break on the stones with the sound of hammers

Cockerel

Vain cockerel
This morning shrilled yankee-doodle-dandy on a victory
     pile !
He wears ten uniforms – draped in as many colours as a
     garrison church
Stiff with embroidered battles

I throw a handful of peanuts
He scrabbles for them with the hens
Each time he gets a peanut in his beak
He groans and drops it at some chick's feet
Only twice is he able to turn his back on his harem
And gobble his peanut

Perhaps in the morning when he chanticleers from his dung
     steeple
He's weak with hunger
I look into his bright eye
Doesnt he know the price of glory ?

A Dog

For sixteen years she went with me
She did not learn to walk but ran or danced till she was old
Then she loitered or stood still
And looked at the world as though she wasnt in it
But saw it as a field beyond a gateway
A good working dog yet till she died strangers called her
    puppy
She ate and slept and managed things simply
Rebukes dismayed her
But at one friendly sign everything was right
No recriminations – she didnt remember that something had
    been wrong
It was hard for her to lose interest
Till one day she walked out in the drizzle
And the force of the drops knocked her over
In a minute she was dead
Having finished with life

Fantails

This year three times the true pair bred
First sudden ice in April
Next a worm in the bud
Then early one morning the grey tree-rat
Came bouncing along the branch
And ate their young ten days in the world
Now new eggs
Laid in two places

Pigs

The oblong van wide open at one end
As if the gate of hell was a side of the world
The pigs come from a concrete field or cement slab
Crippled at birth and killed later
On a metal grid strewn with excrement
Now they come down the gangway
Delicate on tiny feet
Brows wrinkled in puzzled expectation
As living things face their future
On the plate food for the buyers and sellers
At the end of the meal the plate is empty
And in the market the price of hunger rises
Men do not starve by bread alone

On a Friend's Suicide

1.
At times over the five days before
He squeezed his throat with his fingers and thumbs
First he watched in the window – the roofs and trees beyond –
    pain in the front gardens
Then in the mirror – pain confined to a line round his neck
So he could

Then he hanged from a nail like an empty picture frame

2.
Touch the earth gently
The child's foot can kick mountains into the sea
Yet armies march over it and the wind from our banners
    sweeps dust from the ruins

When we passed was our nod too careless ?
When you were not at our side we thought you'd fallen back
   to rest
In the new world you could have built your house
But you are buried in the old world
Which is a place of graves where often the good is damned
   and wasted
In this world where could you build your house ?
You were a child who played on mountains

Touch the earth gently – it is a place of armies and children
   and the wind of banners and ruins

3.
Yes it can be thrown away and if not its taken
So what is the waiting for ?
The work with blunt tools ?
The labour not shared with comrades ?
To sit at the doors of offices where little minds feed big
   bellies ?
To be swindled by placemen and abused by uniforms ?
To see love shrivel and hear the arrogant chatter of poor
   threadbare apes ?

It can be thrown away or taken
Yet we should keep photographs of our enemies
Walk over continents to pick up the lame child
Talk to the silent woman by the river
Above the shout of the crowd hear the city's sighs
And do and say the things that change the world
So that we know peace and days that go well
And as the hare leaps in snow and eats grass
Live till we're taken and prosper till we fall

On a Dead Writer

You who survived the time of the murderers
Killed yourself
I see you standing up to your waist in the Styx
I call – you do not look up or answer
So urgently are you writing all that you had to tell
But you write on water
When you end a word the beginning has been washed away
That is the fate of poets who die by their own hand
With their death they take our inheritance into the grave

To a Friend

It is said that friendship has no end
The handshake's warmth cannot leave the universe
But keeps the frost from an early flower or tempers the wind
It is said no sound dies but travels in space as time passes to
    its limits
So that if one day people can hear all that we said
Perhaps they will not learn most from our orations
But from an aside we forgot as soon as we'd made it

Eclipse of the Sun

An old woman walked on her garden path
To see the eclipse of the sun
Announced in the papers
Slowly the black fist filled the white face
Then as if it was a conjuror's hand
A great white crown sprang from its blackness
The old woman stood on the path and watched
Till voices called from the kitchen

Cancer Ward

You sit propped in bed
Lollipop woman with a shaved head
I have seen those anxious eyes
In cornered rabbits
Death licks your bare arms to taste what's to come
Your husband: shirt and wool tie sits on the bed
Out in the ambulance yard
Pigeons coo and strut and manoeuvre for roosts
On the giant heating duct

Old Man in the Garden

He lies in a canvas chair wrapped in a shawl
His feet stretched before him
He nods – wind turns the pages as if a giant read over his
    shoulder
He wakes – children play in the neighbouring field
He looks at the mottled toad-skin on the hands in his lap

When I was a youngster I built towers of sticks and stones
I've lived in most of a century that's almost ended
I shut my eyes – sun on my face
I sleep so well in this garden
In the thin barrier of grass

When I'm dead friends will kiss me
My face will touch their face
Death isnt a friend or an enemy
We come and go

There will be a feast and flowers
But my house will not be my house
At least I wont have to hear the speeches
Death is neither a friend nor an enemy
I sleep so well in this old garden
In my barrier of grass

On Seeing a Man Fall Through Ice

The ice shone in late afternoon sun
Ridges of hoar-frost scuffed up by skates
In wars and on tightropes skill is only the edge of clumsiness
The ice broke and the skater fell
The black water didnt reflect the light
Or a hand reach from it for the side of the hole
Perhaps the cold had stunned him
Or his scarf tied him to the bottom
Or he swam away from the hole as he tried to swim to it
Some of the skaters kicked at the sides of the hole to make it
   bigger
Some made more holes hacking away the ice at their feet
Old people on the banks shouted warnings: the weight of the
   crowd could capsize the ice
The lifebelt floated like the empty frame of a wreath
When the ice melted frogmen found the body stuck in the
   mud
It had tried to claw its way through the bank

Moon and Day

1. The Child to the Philosopher
The child said
'I would be like the sun and moon and stars
To see all things yet not fall but keep my way'
The philosopher stooped
So that the end of his beard covered the ground
And his cloak lay in folds over his feet
And the ants that hurried along the hem were like broken
    stitches
'Child the sun and moon and stars are barren fields where
    nothing grows'
He turned and walked away
The back of his head was the stump of a signpost
When the way-signs are lost

2. Young Men Look at the Moon
Young men look at the naked moon
Its light fills the earth with skin
The fox crosses a path but does not ponder the nature of
    being
It glides through the empty cages of brambles
Rain drips from the stag's antlers as it walks from the earth-
    lit clearing into the trees
Beside the fire the apple spits and gives out its ripe smell
Before they die young men take off their shoes and walk on
    the moon

3. Who Told You My Name ?
Why does the young moon whisper to me in the forest ?
You are far away yet I hear though you call so softly
Your voice seems to come from the hair on the pillow
If I reach will I touch you ?
If you lie with me I wont let you go
All day I'll hold your hand
The government will be out of order
The customs officers will stop us at the city gate
They wont know how to address the moon
Perhaps they will leave us alone

4. *Moon*
High over the snowfield – trees hedges houses – black
  shadows with sharp edges
The moon
The moon is part of the earth not the sky
The marks on its face do not disfigure it – footprints show
  that a floor is used
In its light the smoke from factory chimneys shines as eerily
  as torches in a crypt – the machines beat as orderly as
  statues' lungs
Nets cast to dry on the mole are full of knives trawled from
  battlefields
Sentries on missile sites huddled in greatcoats stare at her
  nakedness
An ape taught to turn pages still knows at a glance if its new
  master is cruel
The clock-winder's hands turn back at each turn – the moon
  does not turn back
Once the constable of the watch held a lantern over his little
  crew hidden in cloaks
Now from the white sleeve a dark arm rises to hold
The moon over the fields

5. *Sleep*
Window pane
Rain-streaks outside and moisture inside glitter sharply on
  the dark glass
A patch of moonlight in the huge debris of clouds
On the floor at the foot of the bed a heap of clothes

I lie
Under the clay pantiles
In a room as big as an orchard
With walls as thick as barns
A dark stream passes the corner of the house
Over it arch dark bridges of water

An iron bell larger than ten cathedrals
Floats upside down on the sea and rocks in the waves
The iron clapper sways over my head
And comes to rest on the iron walls
Its chant tolls with the sea
I know I am asleep

6. The House
In a room big enough for a kitchen or bedroom
Without a table or bed or cooker or tap or power-point
A small door and a window that looks through a narrow
    chasm between brick walls into a little garden
On the floor some standard-length planks and a stack of
    bricks
Some of the planks are leant on the bricks
And there are paintpots and nailbags and packets of size
Clutches of tubes of lining paper with dented ends
And glass panes with glistening lips
And out on the laurels a thin sprinkling of snow that cant be
    mistaken for light
We build the house but sometimes we are like words that
    dont know the alphabet in which they're written
In the room a smell of turned earth and the shed where the
    planks were sawn and planed

7. Summer Nights
Summer nights are never dark
Twilight stays and day comes slowly
A dog sleeps with the edges of its eyes awake
So with summer nights
Even when there is no moon the clouds are clear
Dawn does not come only at the horizon
It comes from the roof of the sky
As if day rose from the whole earth

8. Day
She bends at the door and her skirt covers her feet as she
    pulls at her slippers
She straightens and walks to the east
The gentle wind opens her skirt and her slippers shine in the
    floor
She climbs to the roof and looks at the sky
And everywhere her daughters get out of bed and cover their
    feet
And go through the house to the window or door and
    welcome their mother
Then food is brought to the table and the children are called
    and the day begins

A Child on a Bridge

On a bridge a child crossing the frozen river
White fields – black hedges and trees – grey ice and sky
The wind sounds surprised as it comes over the bank
The child stops and watches a blackman play in the snow
He asks in his head
Why dont the snowballs melt in his hand ?

The Vulcanised Glove

A child has found an old vulcanised labouring glove
Red
The cuff grimy with sweat
On the back of the hand a flap of torn skin
The fingertips worn smooth and white
One finger split up the side
The child sits on the pavement and plays
He picks up the glove by a finger – it waves as if it was on
    the hand of an invisible man going away
He sticks his own hand – thin white as delicate as herring's
    bones – into the dark hole
Two fingers the legs of a puppet
Suddenly the glove runs away over the ground
Fast

The Red Beard

On the river bank a boy and two girls fish and play
November – grey water – brisk wind
White jostling wave-tops as jagged as broken crockery
There – in the quick current – something red
The rod swings – fishes it out
A beard
Tight curls of the red plastic wire used in saucepan scourers –
    not water-logged
The children stare at it in the muddy grass

Teatime – they cycle home on the tarmac path
The town's smoking chimneys
Streets of eating and beds and string and scissors and paper
Where children sometimes walk away from a game
Upstream a travelling circus or show ?
Or a lost toy detective set: handcuffs – crime notebook –
    fingerprint chart – disguises ?
The earth half sticks out of an envelope
They could have thrown the beard and let the river carry it
    off to sea
Now it lies in the grass

Web

God watching a fly in the spider's web
Comes to no conclusion
The empty web disturbs me
I see men falling from the sky
Clutching at clouds

Winter

Leaves have fallen from the branches
Suddenly – nests in the bare trees as if built by ghosts
Ruined summer palaces
Stalls abandoned in the market
Jackets thrown into ditches

Lark Over an Oak

A lark sang over an oak
Of lost joy and the end of freedom
Of men and women already as rigid as death
Their backs to the wall
The oak shuddered as it fell
The leaves flew away
The roots gripped the soil like hands on bars
The earth dropped
And left the lark singing in nowhere
But all who heard it sing over the oak
Go through ten doors
To a new world

The Roof of the House

On the roof of the house
The weathervane's spear points into the wind
Be alert to your enemies
If the tree bends too often
It is deformed or uprooted
In season the tide turns with the wind
And the world is often in season

Lilac

The mendicant spring has haunted the house for weeks
Dressed in the rags of winter
Begging the scraps of summer
Today the purple lilac opened
Through the rags the ripeness of harvest
I thought of the bright headscarves of women
Stooping in the fields last summer

Lark

At evening I see you pale
Against clouds dark with rain
Above the fields of green corn
You sing in your high estate over us
And in the field beyond
A tractor murmurs quietly
A lover on a woman
Lark ! you still rise in our century

Morning Sky

High mackerel clouds
Strands of white on blue – rucked bedsheets
A bee drones in the grass
The wind is as faint as breath across a room
The earth watches over the sleeping sky
And at night children lie in their bunks
With their arms and legs in the gestures of dancing
Outside the street is silent
In the room there is gentle breathing
And we watch over their deep sleep

Sonnet

He was a tall man with huge hands
He let few people get close
But warned off the rest with courtesy
His grey hair was cropped
He smelt of brick dust
He would cadge a cigarette
He once built a shower in a chimney
He'd crouch in the hearth and rinse himself
And sometimes he heard his mother's voice in the chimney
Telling him secrets – it was the wind in the stack
He carved a father who told the law in the form of fables
And a woman who holds her son after a street accident and
    hears the ambulance wail
He had been a mystery to his mother long before she died
Michelangelo

Greek Island

Hot marble the colour of flesh
Stones as still as resting runners
Dry grass moving like slow water
Air like girls' hair tied in blue scarves

Lokum

Between Lokum and the mainland
Light from the full moon
Falls on the strait
The fisherman wipes his hand on the patch
His wife stitched this morning

In the Morning We Lay Together

In the morning we lay together after we'd made love
I said to myself
This afternoon I shall make love to you
As she came from throwing crumbs to the sparrows
I said to myself
This afternoon I shall make love to you
As she laughed while she read the newspaper leader
I said to myself
This afternoon I shall make love to you
As I watched the ends of her jeans touch her calves
I said to myself
This afternoon I shall make love to you
As I heard her footsteps in the hall
I said
This afternoon I shall make love to you
When her car door banged as she returned from visiting
    friends
I said
This afternoon I shall make love to you
As she pulled the cork from the bottle with her teeth and
    smelt the vinegar
I said to myself
This afternoon I shall make love to you
As she stared at the glasses with their dregs and the plates
    littered with scraps of food and the tray on which we'd
    heaped the left-over food for tomorrow
I said to myself
This afternoon I shall make love to you
And when it was afternoon we went to bed and made love
And now that I notice other things I see it is evening
And the lamps have been lit on the fishing boats going to sea

Market

She stole my wife from my side
At six in the morning
To take her down to the harbour market
In time for the pick of the vegetables
And its true that I would be sorry
If the vegetables were old

A Hair

As I entered her flesh
There was a hair of hers
Her left my right
That asked a question
A mouthless tongue in a tongueless mouth
And a mouth that smiles before it is born to question

Snoring

Half-way through the night she snores
Breathes in – the rattle of a cart on a cobbled hill
Breathes out – a sigh half as long as the rattle
I take her hand in mine

Street Poem

The sky was grey
The clouds hung down like cobwebs
I walked along the street and in my head
I added up the bills – I needed time to pay
The autumn leaves were smeared with city grime
And in the little park littered with papers
Retailing wars and racism and crime
The flowers stared with haggard faces
And then I saw ten milk bottles in a line
On the stone doorstep of a house
And laughed aloud in joy
The cat had lapped its milk
Children had sucked through straws
And neighbours gossiped over cups of tea
The bottles were half-rinsed – a busy housewife
The pale sun shone on glass dirty with white
And my heart leaped at the sight

The Wissey

The Wissey

Botany Bay

I left my wife for a week while she cared for my mother
Who is my mother and not my mother
And my nephew who is like me and not like me
To write on a boat

That evening an old man in a yellow shirt
Passed on the bank with a boy and a leash of three whippets
And at the water's edge two coots stood on their nest of grass
   and reeds
And gazed into the water
Their face-shields as white as moons

I was alone on the river with that sorrow
Which is more than one person's sorrow but is not despair
Ancient sages named the stars after gods and wonders
The fen people named this mooring Botany Bay after the
   convict settlement
To which their parents and children were shipped
They did not see them again
They used the earth to record their sorrow
Which is more than one person's sorrow
As if the earth was their book

Cattle

In the low hollow behind the bank
Cattle pass the mooring six times a day
Or sometimes stand vacantly staring
Or lie like rocks chewing the grass that grows on them
Mostly I see their mouths close to the ground
Tearing at food

They stare as I come
Flies spin round their eyes
Coats matted with excrement
At the last moment they flinch and veer away
Or stumble to their feet
They are big enough to kill me

Even halfway through the night
When I climb the bank they drift
Black clouds on the earth
And I hear them patiently
Tearing and tearing and tearing at grass

In hot summers before I was born
Between hedges heavy with fruit
As birds sang men marched whistling
To be killed like cattle

Long ago and it doesnt trouble my dreams
But some nights I wake and think of the cattle
Who honoured their butchers
And the women who each week gave thanks
For a few shillings pension
Is the mind corrupt
That it can hold such evil ?

Perhaps when our lives are ended
Men will honour themselves and each other
Not give the knife and their neck to the butcher
Cattle with gravestones of grass

And the work and offal and slaughter
Will change the world
So that those who wake at night
Will not lie in terror at being human
But give thanks to be numbered among them

Grandparents' House

In my childhood even the green corn was ripe
Thousands of butterflies flew on the grass banks
In the early morning the women hurried about the kitchen
The primus noisily cooked the breakfast eel
Caught the night before in the chickenwire trap
My grandfather hung in the cut at the end of the garden
The men went to work in the fields
The horses fed from a jingling feed-bag tied to their face
At night I slept under the roof
In the stillness of stars

Grandparents

My grandmother was pear-shaped
Fat hung from her shoulders
She had twelve children
When they were bad she put them under the kitchen table
Three times on the sabbath she and my grandfather walked
    to the fen chapel built of red corrugated iron
Their children walked behind them – there and back it was
    seven miles

Her grey eyes were shaped like links in a chain
A little woman with only her own strength for authority
She conversed as if she was making decisions and giving
    orders
I never heard her row with her husband
She was harsh but not cruel
She used her hands to wash children not hit them
She was a moth inside the window fighting to reach the
    garden
I was too young to recall when I first saw her
I last saw her in hospital when her husband was dead
She knew she'd been taken there to die: she'd often packed
    her sons' sandwiches on the mornings they herded cows
    into lorries
She sat up in bed in a heap of white pillows
And scolded her daughters when they made their visits
It was a joy to hear her winkle out facts and pass the
    judgements and warnings she'd learned in her long
    dealings with traders and landowners
Her daughters presented their jam sponges and told how
    many eggs they'd put in the mixture
They asked the nurses to slice them and share them out in
    the ward and noisily insisted there was enough for all and
    all should be treated alike
It was the way they showed her they were good daughters
I always thought of my grandfather as old
He was thin
He had crinkly hair
On sunday mornings he sharpened his tableknife on the back
    doorstep
It had a yellow bone handle and the blade was honed to a
    thin triangle
No one else was permitted to use it
He sliced his batter-pudding with long careful strokes and
    ate it with thick gravy before the meat and potatoes and
    greens were served
I watched him chew slowly and his eyes focus on space as he
    pondered the taste
On sunday afternoons with the same knife he cut slivers from
    a wad of moist tobacco

Then sat in his white shirt-sleeves and silk-backed waistcoat
and smoked
The stem and bowl of his pipe were black
On weekdays as he could not afford tobacco he sucked at the
empty pipe
He made my grandmother flyswats from a length of wire and
a strip cut from the leg of a wellington boot
When he was old she couldnt cope with his incontinence
His daughters had moved to the towns – they said it would
be cruel to take him from the surroundings he knew
So he was put in a large doll's house
I saw him with other old gentlemen – the old ladies were
kept separate –
Each in a high-back chair with a wooden tray fastened over
the front
Which stopped them from wandering off or falling out and
could be used as a stand for their white mugs
The chairs were set in a row round the walls facing inwards
The rest of the room was for staff and visitors
I gave him a wad of tobacco
My hand smelt for days
He made no sound during our visit after the greetings
There was a whimpering expression on his face
His daughters spoke kindly to him as if he was a child and
after a silence answered their own questions in the second
person
He knew he should not have been there
He had nothing to leave
He left nothing

Shippea Hill

When the trains stopped in the station we called to the yanks
    in blue uniforms
Who leant from the carriage windows
'Got any gum chum ?'
Sometimes they gave us a thin flat stick wrapped in silver foil
Later when they flew low along the track to practise straffing
    runs
They passed so close to the house I saw their jaws move
I could have touched their planes as if they were my toys

March

Grey days when drowned sailors walk the streets
Hunched in black clothes and hands deep in their jacket
    pockets
Days of roaring winds and white clouds racing in blue sky
So much coming and going – chopping and changing –
    laughter out of place – tears for what cant be avoided –
    hands shaking or clutching the head
Sentiment making the trivial important and the important
    trivial
You'd think april would never come
But it does

A sensible traveller shields his eyes against explosions
A careful father plugs the roof with rags and rolled-up plastic
    bags
A wise mother stands the pram away from the window
The window-frame doesnt fit – why should the builders work
    well ? – we measure in profit not kids !

In march starlings find their hole in the tree and rebuild
  their nest
Day after day daffodils unravel their green knot
Their heads dont look up but across to the town
Its true the celandine stares stupidly at the sky
But it grows close to the ground – from there you have to
  look up
And at night it closes itself against intruders and the rain
  runs off its shiny roof
I trust the earth to the seasons
Its creatures endure and grow

Raid

At six I saw
Small men
Gather in crowds
Like heaps of stones
Or run crouched
In the streets
Or into corners

Over them men
In goggles and helmets
Hunting like dogs
Backwards and forwards
In the gaps between searchlights
Press buttons
And death screams down

A small plane
Trapped in the light
Like a fly on flypaper
With the guns onto it

Then I no longer
Asked about men
But what wind blew this terror
Into the dark sky ?
And when they rejoiced at victory
I asked how long ?
And how is the house made safe ?

In these nights
Children learn
Their fathers are children
And weep that the world
Is a ball
Blown by wind through empty streets
Till in time
They have care of the world

The Wissey

From time to time on still days
A breath of wind suddenly turns the top of the river
To shining silver
As if it spread a carpet
For a girl to walk on to the boat
It might have been said
This was the water from which Venus was born
Lifted many times to the clouds
And dropped on this fen sluice
If Venus had been born from the Cyprus sea
But who is to say it is not the water in which the Trojan
    women pounded bedclothes and uniforms and washed
    their dead
And later their prison steps
Years after the soldiers had hacked themselves to pieces in
    their workroom
Throwing their blood down on the threads in the looms
In the afternoon that made the world modern ?

April

In a book a picture – a sword hilt – on it a steel rose shaped
    like an eye in a bed of steel leaves
Some dreams are cast in steel
But the mind is always in migration
When the pasture is grazed the herdsmen move on
Iron boats float under the bridge that carries traffic to the
    city
Philosophers' fingers drum empty pages like the blind
    looking for braille
The garden rosebud – one touch and the flower is crippled
But touch the steel rose more gently
It does not live in its own scented air

Sounds

Very early in the morning
Small sounds round the boat
Mooring ropes sigh – the canvas flaps
On this stretch of river three moorhens nest – sharp little
    kitchen-chatter calls as if they fetched milk from the
    doorstep and got ready for work
A little wind passes by on its own
Sounds an infant makes as it talks to itself and kicks its legs
    in the cot
And the day begins

Bomb Runs

All day the NATO terror jets practise bomb runs
Low over houses and fields – you can see the pilots' fingers
The villagers dont look up anymore
If the planes scorched the sky each time they passed they'd
　　blot out the sun in a week
The villagers would grope along the sides of their houses to
　　ask their neighbours what had become of their sun
For they still have houses

The Cuckoo

Each day for hours this spring
The cuckoo called from the wood
Across the river
Two notes like a bell at a prison gate
Or weeping in a madhouse
That proclaim her a robber
And killer of young
And deep in the wood the cuckoos answer

You'd think they'd keep quiet
But then
Brass bands have been used to keep secrets

Armaments Workers

On the radio the armaments minister tells the armaments
　　workers
The air-torpedo contracts will be renewed
The armaments workers cheer
To feed their families they will make air-torpedoes to orphan
　　other families
And now the contracts to make air-torpedoes of the fathers of
　　the other families will also be renewed

The humourless smile of irony doesnt click onto my face
Instead I ask why contracts are made with enemies against
    friends ?
The workers must feed their children
The minister is addicted to victory
And on the stock exchange fortunes must be made for
    air-torpedoes to defend

Night on the Wissey

Autumn
Slight mist
The still river faithfully reflects the orange moon
This afternoon a fish was hauled on a line over the river
    leaving a silver track like a mad water-skier
The fisherman took up his knife
And howled
Now deep below me the reflection is still

September

These quiet days of early autumn are the best
Things can be looked at straight
No need to shade the eyes and no late summer mists
On these days the wind blows them away and dries the grass
The river puckers in perplexity but it will outlive the icy
    tomb
Because the leaves are strong and stay late on the trees they
    will grow new leaves when the old leaves are dead
The small crumpled leaves still wave on the brambles – they
    are like the hands of a party of school children
If I see anyone frowning I nod or show them a calm face
And they pass on reassured

Late Swallows

Each year you fret that the north wind will kill the swallows
    who stay late
These are the young swallows !
They practise coasting the winds and strengthen their wings
    before setting out
How else could they reach the south ?
Greyhead be patient !
The swallows are not making mistakes
But learning

October

A swallow skims over the water
It turns three feet from my face
October wind roars in the poplars and cracked willows
Evening clouds dark with rain
The low sun hangs on a bush a gold collar set with brilliant
    rubies
Flocks of gulls returning to a distant lake rise and fall in the
    wind over the fen as if they crossed mountains
From the bank – at this distance – I seem to look down on
    them
Cattle come to graze the thick grass
A black bullock pushes down the steep slope to the reeds
It stands knee-deep in the water
For a moment it turns to gaze
At the dappled cow that clambers down to its side
Then lowers its head again to drink
It does not know the butcher and I am not troubled by death
The river is at peace

Lorry

Round the still boat
The dark
No wind
No waves
No reeds scratch the hull
Seldom such stillness and silence and darkness
Then far away a sound like the whine of a gnat
The craters just wars make in the face are as deep as the
    craters made by wars that are unjust
Some truths shock those who tell them: let them be silent for
    a while
When they speak again others will speak in their mouth so
    that they wonder at what they know

In the Dark Forest

In the Dark Forest

On Answering Cries

You who jump into the river to rescue someone
Who cries help
May find he struggles so hard to live
He strikes at you like an enemy
So that you both drown
When you answer the cry for help
Remember your own weakness
Remember it in all you do

Deciding

Difficult to decide ? To know what you want ?
How can the puppet tell what the master's hands will do
      next ?
Some decisions are considered painstakingly – then you do
      what's best
The others ? Do it ! – then you learn who you are
These are the decisions by which you live

Going to Work

Sometimes I think I'd like to go
To the shed in my garden each morning and write
Instead I cross the bridge to the theatre
Thought is solitary
It would even hide from itself
Sometimes it is better to study with artists
And learn the subtleties taught in the crowd

The Past

There are writers certain
That what they write is true enough to be underlined
And dictators who underline their small talk with corpses
I take the opportunity this gives me to say
The past is a parasite we should fear

Original Sin

God said Eve plucked from the tree an apple to tempt Adam
Any god who said that was naïve in the ways of the world
His scribe who worked for wages could have told him
Short-supply goods create their own prices
Adam tempted Eve more sorely than Eve tempted Adam
Adam stripped the apples from every apple tree and sold
    them to purchase Eve
Adam who was a farmer plucked a gold coin from his pocket
    and soiled Eve by measuring her in money
Now it is evening
And the shadows fall away from the sun and point
To the place where it rises

The Audience

Some see a bait and run into a snare
Others nod as the snare shuts
Those in the snare shuffle uneasily in their seats
I wrote one play but each audience is many
I did not make a snare or scatter bait
I told the truth as I saw it

On the Shore After Writing

I walked on the shore
What to write ?
The sea has not been silent since the creation yet says
    nothing
It is the unceasing hammer
Those who work with hammers must shout to be heard
Suddenly a shank flies up from the sand
With a sound that is calm and tuneful
And that was a shout of alarm !

Productivity

Apple tree where are your apples ?
You have heard of banana trees in distant lands that grow
    pale fruit
But you remember when you were a sapling and heard the
    market-stalls tell tales of hairy gourds and star-fruit and
    mangoes
And pawpaws named like a dog but with a taste so refined
    and artificial it might have been made by a confectioner
Some fruits are brighter than jade
But pale bananas give a good meal

Apple tree where are your apples ?
You have heard that somewhere a tree with honey-coloured
    pears sweats nectar so sweet that swarms of wasps come to
    pillage
Does it matter ? – children who pick pears can brush away
    wasps
And a worm in the flesh can be cut out

On the track below you there is a blackberry bush notorious
    for its thorns
But the blackberry pickers' fingers arent torn by thorns but
    stained by blackberry juice
They avoid the thorns as skilfully as commandos dodge
    barbed wire
And one of your apples might fall on a Newton's head

Apple tree let your branches be weighed down by apples !
Even if they are sour – grow them !
Green apples are good for thirst
If so little sun shines into this narrow track that your apples
    stay green
Passers-by will stuff those they dont eat into their pockets
    and take them to where the sun shines more often
Those who need fruit know how to make it ripen

In the Dark Forest

In the dark forest
The wolves silently circle in front of their lair
Like a mob of riderless horses

In the dark forest
Trees stand as thick as cages filled with bars
The wolves glide between them as easily as shadows with
    eyes

In the dark forest
The wolfteeth flash
They are sharpened on wolves and cleaned on men

In the dark forest
The spittle that falls from the wolfjaws is blood-shaped

In the dark forest
The wolves howl their slogans at the night

In the dark forest
Frightened birds crash in the treetops
And flutter on the ground

In the dark forest
Wolves use the paths beaten by wolves and men

In the dark forest
Paws fall on the paths as softly as fingers on latches

In the dark forest
In puddles in pawmarks the moon lies ready for the autopsy

In the dark forest
Handtorches stare at each other

In the dark forest
The wolves move closer to the house

In the dark forest
The canopy is thick and dawn does not come at dawn
No day no night

In the dark forest
The beginning is as far away as the end
The future is as lost as the past
Prisoners are always in mid-sentence

In the dark forest
The wolves come on time

Distant Orchard

Suddenly over the ploughed field
Dried by wind
Too soon for spring I saw
Against a sombre sky
Branches in sunlight
The shapes of lightning
Or wire-sea on the Somme
Covered in white
Before leaves and blossom grew
As I drove by

Nativity Poem
(For Loren)

Mid-January
Those thick green stalks in the grass are the tips of
    snowdrops
Yesterday rain washed the snow from the fields round the
    house and the boy was born
Today more people will lose their work and the stock
    exchange index will rise
That doesn't concern him
But when he is older he may find the world so beautiful he
    forgets to think of such things
So I write this today to remind him

London

It seemed autumn would come late to the London street
The leaves stayed green
Suddenly in three days they have shrivelled
But on the ends of twigs close to the top
A few green leaves are left
They dont seem to know the desolation beneath them
    although their dead sisters hurl by them through the air
Here as elsewhere winter comes on time

Beautiful People

On the walls of your houses grow beautiful leaves
How will you escape ?
The government pastes pronuncimentos on walls
Sentries wait out their watch on walls
Prisoners are shot on walls
But leaves can make even prison walls beautiful
In autumn your leaves turn fiery red – can you take a hint ?
And tear down the wallpaper in your lounge
Its even got roses !

Pleasant Landscape

Far fens – sun on fields and tree tops
Everywhere things grow – the sign of the human hand
The silos are not seen till you're close
Along the roads on the wire fences lick-'n-spit neat warning
    signs with skulls and red letters
The rags and bones on the wire at Auschwitz

Music of the Spheres

After the disaster when we lay in ruins
It would be good if people from another world
Who had read on their instruments
The signs of our madness
And had imagined our misery and despair
Broadcast – since they could never visit a place so
    contaminated –
Music through space
So that we knew there were still people who lived in peace
And were not led to death by their rabble of leaders
And be comforted by this human music of the spheres

The University

1. Starlings
Walking in Wivenhoe Wood I heard from the garrison
    beyond the university
Machine-guns rattle
Next time I walked in the wood the machine guns were silent
But the rattle came faintly from the trees
The starlings had learned to imitate machine guns
I went down to the lecture block
Since then nights have closed the skies like caretakers and
    days opened them like cleaners sweeping the steps
But no inquest has been held

2. The Park

The greeks gave hospitality to strangers
When the milestones are open doors the journey is easier
Then even the north wind seems human – it seeks the south
Those who built the tall lecture blocks dont study in them
When the thinkers moved in the workers moved out
Take care of the place till they return
Those who shout fire shouldnt complain that others shout it
    so loudly the firemen wont hear their own shouts
Perhaps those who shout louder are in the burning house
A pity if what unites us keeps us apart
Be as generous as the tree that picks its own fruit for the
    passers-by
Or the stream that gives them its water to wash in and drink

3. The Spear-thrower and the Learned Man

A child teaches itself to walk
Corrected and praised by its elders
But the nature of right and wrong
And the way the world may be understood
Must first be found out by teachers
Then taught to pupils –
How else shall be live ?

What is the learning that will protect us
And allow our cities to prosper ?
First it must explain
That work creates not only useful objects and services
But also our social life
Our institutions and laws and customs
When head works for hand and hand for head
Each in accord with the other
We will live in reason and our values be human
Which is the end of knowledge

Yet when the spear-thrower says to the learned man
'I throw the spear after the swift stag
How shall I build my house ?'
The learned man answers
    'Yes yes juggle the spears over your head !
    High in the air !'

'I throw the spear after the bright fish
How shall I deal in the market ?'
    'Yes yes juggle the spears in the air
    Five ! Six ! Higher ! Faster !'

'I throw the spear at the running enemy
Who is my neighbour ?'
    'Yes yes keep the spears in the air !
    Eleven ! Twelve ! – O best of pupils !'

Guest House

In the TV lobby a circle of salesmen
They are here for a conference on how to sell a practical
    plastic device
On the screen a woman
Her hair is stiffly coiffeured but unkempt – the wig of a doll
    that spends one night in bed and another upside down in a
    shoe-box
Her lips tighten across her teeth in a smile
Her skin is as white as a dust sheet
Her eyes do not cry – others have cried into them
As carefully as someone who mends a radio with a
    thumbnail she speaks of atrocities forty years old
Of women who died on her cell floor
She faces the circle of salesmen who have come to learn how
    to sell a useful plastic device
There are no beggars out in the street
She holds out her empty hand

Frost

In the night a frost
This morning the white park
The canada geese have come to the edge of the parking lot to
    graze the stiff white grass
A businessman sprays de-icer on his windscreen
Very sparingly in the white world

Strange Cities

1.
He stood in the street on a crutch and one leg
The other was crushed by a concrete lump
It was as limp as his blood-soaked trousers before the
    surgeon cut it away
At home frightened children
Even the day wasnt kind but his hat lay on the pavement
The coins in it wouldnt buy one meal
Yet there was something stranger
This man of misery sang songs of young love and roses !
Tell me what strange city it was
Where those in warm coats who hurried to the fourth meal of
    the day
Sighed and muttered as if they were the careworn
While the man of misery sang of young love and roses and
    wine ?

2.

Perhaps in your city children are fed and no lame beggar
  sings in the street
Instead people hurry in silence and on the radio well-spoken
  leaders politely broadcast the howls of a mob
And your children are not frightened by the stories of ogres
  but by the stories you are too frightened to tell them
And you dare not look at the people who wait on the
  corners ?
Is this your city ?
Tell me what strange place I have come to !

Kings Road

Parked on the pavement on the cobbled drive-in to a garage
A car
Inside in the gloom four figures
Suddenly I see uniforms and metal buttons and a red knitted
  beret on top of a skullcap of hospital gauze
Three policemen and a black man
His angry eyes stare like bent bars
From the passers-by he tries to pick out the thugs who struck
  his head with a bottle or kicked it
(He must learn the details from the medical report – most of
  the blows came from behind)
Among those who pass are many who sell the lies that
  assault community
Velvet collars on greatcoats – polka-dot ties – equestrian
  headscarves
Why doesnt he point as they pass ?
Instead the policeman on the pavement steps out of their
  way

Bread With Pictures On It

A worker said each day a man comes to my door
He says work for me and you'll get a living
He gave me bread with pictures on it
I was hungry – now his art's in my stomach
Later I saw the master who teaches my kids
I said I know that face
Then I remembered – that's the man who paints pictures on
    bread
When my mother broke down the doctor also reminded me
    of the bread-painter
I passed the priest's house – a smell of paint and turps
Coming home from school the kids knocked off a copper's
    helmet
The head came off with it – the expression didnt change – it
    was the bread-painter's head
I'd like to know what goes on
I buy my mind on the instalment plan – will I ever get it
    together ?
I dont know my own face in the mirror
Or why my hands are heavier when they're empty
I dont think the bread with pictures does me any good !
The starving should learn to vomit

Reform

The minister of prisons decrees new privileges
Prison library books may be borrowed for three (was two)
    weeks
Coloured socks provided by non-inmates may be worn (on
    feet only) but government-issue socks may not be dyed
    (risk of damage to government property)
The playing of musical instruments may be studied (where
    working instruments are not available cardboard mock-
    ups may be provided)
Caged birds permitted in cells (privilege at governor's
    discretion)
To worshippers attending sabbath chapel extra fifteen
    minutes tobacco time (after the blessing)
All corridors rooms and other interior areas used by
    prisoners' visitors to be painted green (provision not
    extended to cells)
The prisoners are grateful – each day the sun will shine on
    the bars five minutes longer
But the minister for prisons has not given the prisoners a key
    to the bulldozer
Or the privilege of painting the walls with slogans
That turn them into the Books of the Law

Withdrawing a Grant from a Bookshop

A man tapping along the street in sunlight
And a woman reading braille in the dark are blind
But how do we know when a nation is blind ?
Street bands play louder
A policeman showing a new gun on TV strokes the muzzle
Certain students wear waistcoats
People cheer till they are hoarse but are afraid to speak
And books are burned

Those who know most words control the city: no one has
    power till he reads
Some power comes from a gun but to make the gun and
    name the target
Words are written
Books are the arsenals of change

In ancient japan the ruler sent a polite note
'Please be so kind . . .' and the receiver opened his stomach
When the nazis raised their hands in the hitler salute we
    knew there would soon be blood on them
Our rulers' hands are clean and their words polite
They do not burn books: they close bookshops
It is a sign

The Olivier Stage (1985)

In this century we learned much that was new
We rushed through space on chairs
Our work changed: once backs bent under weights – now
    fingers press keys
Once tired factory children slept like bundles dropped in
    corners – we study after work and play after study
Our minds work differently
We see astronauts like footprints in space
And when we counted the numbers of those who died in
    dead causes some of us lost our illusions

This new stage is as broad and deep as a town square or city
    junction
Not a drawing-room where teaspoons rattle like lepers' bells
    and taxidermists set dead passions in poses
Or a cold corridor where coroners tell the victims what to
    die of
On this stage the dead may bear witness and the living argue
    with the oracle
Each man and woman may be a crowd

Gestures reach like bridges over the canyons that obstructed
    armies
Eyes move like searchlights mounted on mountains
And the face be a placard – even the strips torn by vandals
    will judder in the wind like tongues !

And here as on all town squares and at all crossroads there is
    a path for the ants and a patch of dust for the sun
And a place for the small events of the day
A woman weighs fruit in a supermarket
A man dozes while he waits for the factory bus
And children playing games with stones tot up their scores
    on pocket computers
On this stage the times could be seen and heard
But because of the times they are not

The Knife

You think you wake me on the grindstone
I was awake
The screeching tells me things it stops you hearing
You hold me before you like a sleep-walker holding his
    empty hands or a child its toy
There is grit on my blade as if I sweated granite

I enter the house
Cut the pipes for water and gas
Rip the electric cables
I am the shark that swims in the flooded streets
I am the weathervane that points away from the storm
The blood I destroy eases my passage
I go deep
I journey like a city mob that dwindles to hermits scattering
    over a desert
I could be labelled and put in a case with the knife that
    killed caesar
You throw me away in the street

A bullet goes through its target and flattens itself on the wall
A bomb destroys itself in its explosion
A rope frays like old hair whether its used to bind or break
But what was in me is always in me
I cut hawsers and store-bales and dressings for wounds
Slice bread and act in proverbs
I am the foundations of hamlets and cities
Hold me – do not be afraid
I come from a proud line
I fit your hand and belong
I am finger-shaped

The Iron People

I have been asked to write a poem
To be sent with other poems in support of disarmament
To a woman who boasts she is an iron lady

When the scientists at Los Alamos were told their bomb had
    destroyed Hiroshima they cheered
That night you had to tip the head waiter if you wanted a
    table in the best local restaurants
Genghis Khan dined on a stage raised over a mound of his
    dead and dying foes
And the commandant of Auschwitz delighted in counting
    heads
These are commonplaces of depravity
But as it is said Field Marshal Haigh wept when he first saw
    the trenches
Though unfortunately the war had ended by then
Perhaps there is a chance that the mind of a woman who
    boasts she is made of the same metal as bombs
Might be changed by a poem – if it was good enough ?

No – iron people are not changed by poems or reason
Write for those who weep before wars not after: by then
    they're dead
In the great war the sound of the Flanders barrage was
    heard in Whitehall
In the iron lady's war the wailing will come to us over seas
    and continents
And as we die we shall hear – if for a moment we are quiet –
    our victims' last cries
So that in this way the iron lady may boast she let the news
    of our victory reach us in time
For us to die happy

Before we can get rid of bombs we must get rid of iron people

Grand Hotel

After the hotel had been bombed the ministers appeared on
    TV
In the days before we had seen them stabbing the air with
    their fingers as they threatened strikers
Even as they claimed to be creating new jobs the number of
    jobless rose to a record
With arguments unchanged since they won the school
    debating society cup they demanded that workers obey the
    laws they passed to protect their own power
The malice of these collar-and-tie thugs set the conference
    audience squealing and stamping
This was the ruling class in the indian summer of power
We wondered how such people could rule
Perhaps it is all a matter of arrogance ? – the vehemence
    with which the young public-school nazi on the podium
    calls the strikers' leader a thug
And now they have been bombed

We saw the hotel's gleaming façade: a giant billboard smile
    with a smoking cavity
The minister's face stuck from the rubble: no doubt this was
    pain but the sneer was so habitual no change could be
    noticed
Yet suddenly they are human: they have problems
Today their eyes stare like those of a woman who thinks of
    her unpaid rent
Their faces are as blank as the unemployeds' leaving the job
    centre
Their shoulders as tense as the mother's whose son is on
    active service in the wars of little islands
For once they do not interrupt the interviewer but wait as
    humbly as the wife who sits in the long corridor of the
    victorian hospital while nurses fight to keep her husband
    alive on a support machine twenty years older than the
    metal press that crushed him

Tomorrow their tongues cut from jackboots will rasp as they
    vote money to arm police now that they have another
    reason
And to close hospitals and schools and build prisons and
    military airstrips
But today they sit as meekly as children with cut knees –
    their suits smell of bombdust and they look at the TV
    interviewer as if they hoped he would give them a
    comforting pat on the wrist
These ministers who can appear human only after they have
    been bombed

It Is Easy

O that the iron doors would close on my enemies !
But here you must learn to love the sharp frost
Welcome the bitter wind
Watch with interest the ravelling of the three-nail puzzle
    they call a solution
And calmly wait as your enemy pursues himself
Those left unburied on the parade ground
And the little ranks of panicky children paraded before the
    wolf
Make it easier

Interview

At the end I said to the TV interviewer
One day as we walk in the street
We will see the state of the world and how we live
And burst into tears
And change it

When it was screened they cut out
And change it
And ended with tears
Next time I will cut out the tears

Goya and his Gardener

Goya's gardener went with him at night to the hill
And held the lantern while he drew the dead
And the dying who stirred and sighed as the hungry dogs
    went among them
He asked: Señor why paint the barbarities of men ?
He answered: It makes me happy that even when I am dead
    I shall tell them
Stop being barbarians

I Was Afraid

Goya kept me out of Madrid
I was afraid of the disasters and follies
Till one summer when I worked there
I went to the Prado
And found that reason is strong
And nothing will be hidden
And in the street I said
We do not fight just because we are attacked
But because we know joy

It Is a Joy to Be With the Noble and Good
(From the Dhammapada)

It is a joy to be with the candid and honest
If you never had to be with fools
Perhaps you would always be happy

The days of those who work beside fools
Are miserable and long
To be with fools is to be with an enemy
You are in pain
But to work with the wise
Is like the joy of greeting good comrades

If you find a teaching that does not go astray when it
    explains change
That is not easily sullied in struggle
That understands communities and individuals
Then study this useful and friendly teaching
As the moon follows the path of the stars

Cuckoo

I stand in my garden
And hear with surprise
That today the call of the cuckoo
Which before I had always thought cruel
Is gentle and kind
For a moment I am perplexed till I understand
Yesterday I was with envious men

Sloane Square

The square is a busy part of the city
A theatre restaurants stores hotels and mews flats
Even at night cars screech round its corners
By day passers-by dont look up at the branches of the tall
    plane trees and the sky's rafters
At night when the offices and shops shut they hurry not to be
    late for the morning
But just before dawn
For fifteen minutes the square is silent
As if the stones needed a rest

Sonnet: Who Threw These Toys in the Fire ?

Who threw these toys in the fire ?
Was it a child or the parents ?
The doll's plastic legs bubble and kick
Her yellow tutu burns with a blue flame
A sudden bonfire ! – her blond wig blazes and dies to a black
    stain on the pink coals
The stern of the SS Everfirst juts from the sea at a sinking
    angle
The lego bridge and dinosaur skeleton sag into Lava Lake
A plastic ball with coloured sections like a clown's globe –
    vintage carboots and hot-rod bumpers – soldiers' heads
Who threw these into the fire ?
A child or an adult passing through the room ?

War

I am Priam's son
I return from the field with my hair and hands clotted with
    brothers' and strangers' gore
My sister shouts the truth to the sky in halls with no roofs
    and broken windows and doors hanging from hinges
Out in the street she stops passers-by – they hurry away –
    they take her for a gypsy selling fortunes
In the palace she shouts at war ministers too busy running
    the war to learn who will lose it
My mother sits upright in her crooked bed
She is half stone – and the other half is dogshit at the foot of
    the column
No the top of her body is the gravestone on the festering rest
    of it !
And my father Priam is dead !
No cats or dogs or birds – not even rats
We ate the rats while our dead were in their bowels !
We ate the bark from the trees !
The wide plain between our walls and the enemy fleet doesnt
    have space for the footprints of our funerals !
I am tired – let it end – I long to be silent

Visitors

When they come from a distant world and land on our
    cinders
They will find the fireproof button pressed to fire the rockets
And on it will be a thumbprint
So that they say
    At least humans were here !

See This

After fire had razed the city
When charred bodies smoked
And human dust had not yet settled on the ruins
A woman came to the emergency casualty station
And stepping over the dying and wounded on the pavement
Where babies poked their fingers at dead women's teeth
Reached the front of the crowd and called to a doctor
'Me first – I paid – private patient'
And it was because in the past it had been possible to say
   such things in the city
That it and other cities were burned
   Wherever you build hell fire will find it

This House is Made of Stone

This house is made of stone
Wind blows and the trees bend
Wind blows and the grass bends
Wind blows and the flowers shake
But the stone is not moved
Wind breaks the sky in the pool
The stone still stands
Wind tears the lamb's fleece
The fox in the mouth of its lair narrows its eyes in joy at the
   storm
The stone stands
Wind shears dust from the side of the stone
It stands
Blow harder wind !
And howl at the dust you blow in your face

The Allegory of Canute

Enthroned on the beach Canute said great sea withdraw !
The tide came on
He shivered and spread his beard over his knees
Look said Canute I am frail !
He ran to the high ground – the tide followed him
His empty throne bobbed on the waves
The tide rose to a flood
His castles crumbled into the sea – the land was lost and the
    king drowned
But now he returns at the head of the waves !
Look – the dead king raging with his sceptre ! – riding the
    sea with dead marshals and generals !
Send Canute back !
You are stronger than dead kings and their marshals and
    generals !
You are the human flood !

Do Not Be Dismayed

The world is in chains
Everywhere the tyrant's uniform is paraded
The struggle for freedom may cost you your life but it is
    certain that slavery would cost you your life
Those who dont die fighting the tyrant die fighting for him
Or live in his prisons and forge the chains for their necks
Dont be dismayed ! – the first steps are easy
You dont have to knock down a wall – a hole will do
If you can shovel cement you've already begun to dig up
    your cell floor
If you can forge steel you've already begun to force open the
    links of the chains
After that the struggle will train you

Reflections

When the river flows gently between fields
The stones on the bottom are bright in the clear water
When storms rage in the mountains and the river is in
    torrent
The stones on the bottom are hidden in mud
If you stir water with a stick dont expect it to be clean
Wait till the storm is past and then you may drink
When you pull the oars dont expect the fish to follow the
    boat
Cross and then you may eat
Do you describe the sunset to those who walk under it ?
If they cant see it tell them to stoop
They will find its reflection in the machines on their bench
    and the cups on their table

Dialectic

Water is a cool element
Your hand may find cold hot and hot cold
Heretics are burned in an orthodox fire
Dialectical choices arent made by the toss of a coin
There is no escape from freedom
The runners may not be coming to tend the wounds
But to stitch the holes in the jackets
Watch when the killers prowl
The thugs are armed with knives
The monsters are armed with needle and thread

Struggle

The fisherman's rope
The sheath-binder's cord
The porter's strap
The gaoler's fetters
Simple questions – no simple answers
When the gods cannot bear anymore reality they make a
    miracle – that way we'll always need miracles !
So much for the wisdom of gods !
    Men and women must struggle !

You Who Love Peace

The dove of peace is silent
She cannot sing of victory or lament
Dead soldiers or those they took an oath to save
As they are carried to the grave
Long long ago she lost the power of song
Pleading for those who wept and bled
When wars were games for kings to wage
Over some righteous wrong
But in this democratic age
When people are thrown down
Like the red carpet on agamemnon's stage
You may still hear the clap of wings
As the white bird rises in your dark town
An echo that comes before the sound
Of the thunderbolt
When the sky is buried in the ground
You who love peace sing
Her song at dawn and evening and at noon
Or you will be as silent as the dove that's soon
Cut in stone monuments and tombs
Then ground to dust by bombs

Boots

Asked to walk into a new continent
And it was a continent they had desired
And when the sea desires it can bring forth land
They said: Wait – boots !

Good ! Good !
What fools talk of land without talking of boots ?

Let Me See Summer

Look the apple born in cold spring ripens
Yet here the ranks of classes
Make courage cold and joy bitter
Winter come !
Let me see summer before I am old

It Is All a Question of Power

The gods are dead and the cities and farms are bigger
But I cannot find any wisdom the ancients did not already
    have
Ptahotep said to the poet – listen to the girls at the
    grindstone
When Gilgamesh died they said – but look at his buildings !
And Senshi boasted – I brought the boatless to land

So it is all a question of power
A stone on the ground is one thing and in the wall another
    and in the fist another
Always it was the crooks who made laws and the gods who
    asked miracles of the people
In railway-yards mines factories and housing estates old
    sayings are still heard
But the meaning is new
Truth is not in the words but the speaker
At last those in the ferry and those in the water may call to
    each other – brothers ! sisters !
And the boatless be brought to land

Poor Bastards

When Im shot – no blindfold
Let me see the light of day or the electric bulb
The uniforms and muzzles
Let me look down the wrong end of the gunsights
And hear the stamp of feet and sounds from beyond the walls
    – if my luck's in even voices from the distant city
Dont blindfold me unless it helps the poor bastards ordered
    to shoot

Seven Cycles

Seven Cycles

I Love You

1.
I love you
I look in a mirror and see your face
After a street accident a woman lies in exploded glass
Torn flesh
I dial 999 and think of your flesh
If a woman smiles at me in the street when I'm going to you
Dont think I'll go straight to you
First I go with her
Then come to you
Because I love you

2.
Flash
Explosion
Forest fire starting up in dry grass
Flames licking trees
Branches – drunks fighting with burning whips
Black smoke writhing in white smoke
Trunks grinning with the fire inside them
Rabbits bolting into burrows
Suffocated
Hares like mob victims dashing along walls of fire
Birds flying in furnaces till the heat beats them down
Or rising in smoke and tumbling into flames
Suffocated – no wings – no legs – burned
Bracken cackles
Branches throw fireballs over the river
Trunks fall and lay like bridges – fire runs on them
The forest burns with a steady roar and sudden explosions
Till the flames reach the end of the trees
The silent villagers stand in groups and look over the field
At the mob burning their forest
A wall of fire jumping and hurling threats and insults
The sides of their houses glow
Firelight leaps through the windows
The curtains stir like sleepers in fever

3.
I watch the fly crawl on the newspaper
Over the threats of the secretary of state for defence
And news of an African drought
I contemplate
If when my head was bent in passion
My hand was an inch from your stomach
You said kill Claudio
I would
Or you told me to rob the old money lender Alyouva
    Ivanova
Or enter a café and poison a meth drinker's bottle
Or break a child's hands
I would
When my hand reached that empty inch
I would not contemplate
The fly crosses the printed lines
Troops crawled in trenches with their face in the mud as if
    they bowed to the pure air
I contemplate without fear

4.
Night
I have come through the dark house
Passed the shut doors as still as spies
To stand at your bed
I lift back the sheet
You lie still
Naked
As I open your legs your arms obeying the law of matter will
    fold around me
Your breasts are warm from the sheets
Their warmth is different from the warmth of the rest of your
    body
As I take your nipples in my mouth your neck will stretch
    and the back of your head will slide higher up the pillow
You have given your consenting command
I have escaped to your cell
If the syphilis-man with lipskinned mouth told me your body
    was impure
Or the AIDS ghost came through the wall
I would lie with you
And trust the healing

5.
Your teacup on the table
An open book face down
I stick my tongue deep in the cup and swallow the taste of
    your tea
Where have you hurried away ?
Dont think I'd wait if you dont come back
There are other women
I need flesh so I love you
If there were no flesh there would be no love
But do not doubt it
No one will love you as I love you

6.

The sculptress hits the chisel into the stone with a hammer
You shape my hair
Deepen the cut of my mouth
Chisel pupils into my eyes
My age my gestures the stance of my feet
Follow patterns chosen by you
And knocked through the chisel
I obey as stone obeys the wind that shapes it
Only the blows of wood on steel and the chipping and
     crumbling of stone are heard
The mouth you cut is silent
But blood runs from the lips
In truth I have not seen you for fifteen years
The red veins are in the marble

7.

Yesterday
We sat on the clifftop
Your hair hit your face like curtains flapping in an open
     window
Your body became a house with stories and doors
Passages and rooms to live in
I lay on you
I entered
The town was in earthquake
Walls waved laconically
Minutely recording the shocks that engulfed them
I dug my hands into heaving bricks – held waving floor-
     beams between my legs – tumbled in hoisted streets
The foundations of the sea rose
Now I lie on the fallen ruins
In the peace of those destroyed by chaos
I have cried out
My face has spent its passion
My cheek is on the pavement open to the sun – a few pieces
     of grit press into the skin
It was the best time with your body

8.

Like a ship upside down
I lie on my bed in the barracks
I am naked
My body is not tortured
It tortures me
I am a man dying of thirst who cannot swallow the water in
    his mouth
A mother feels this when her dead child cannot smile at her
I am a trunk with the ivy ripped off
Insects have no salvation – they stare at the sun

I do not pretend you are here
My tears are salt in my eye wounds
I lie still
Once or twice my head turns
I must not panic
These are years like the hyphen cut between dates in stone
I sleep
My body wakes me
It is as relaxed and arrogant as a torturer
It tortures me

9.

I lie on the beach
Naked under the big towel
There is a wind but I am warm
Half asleep I look through closed eyelids
I listen to the sea's groans
I fall into a deep sleep
You swim towards me
You are crying into the ocean
Your tears dry on distant shores
I smile
I wake
Wind ripples the towel
Breakers fall on the beach
The sand under me shakes
I cried while I slept
A few salt tears dry on my face
I do not move
I must start to learn to live without you

10.

The little girl crouched by the river
Yellow vest and blue shorts
Fiddling with something in the grass
Freckles on her forehead and arms
A few on the tops of her thighs
The legs of her shorts are open
I see the carefully folded girl's flesh
I think of you
Young
I wade into the river
Fast water pushes against my hips
You are everywhere

11.

The damsels fly over the river like leaping skiers
The tips of their tails bobbing on the top of the water
Trout jumping at evening flies know only water
They live on the edge of land but never go there
Unless they're hauled through the air on a line
Their wake is still white when the short tackle of knife and
    cloth and hand is over
I can endure hell because I know I am in heaven
But I am tired of pain and wonder if those around me have
    been to heaven ?
How can I trust those who have not been to heaven ?

12.

It was your body
Its surface and shape
Its weight
The pride with which you rested
The openness of your gaze – a white bowl in which things
    vanished
Your satisfaction – like a child conceived in the air entering
    into its mother's body
The simplicity of your passion
The warmth of your hands – the coolness of your feet
Your calmness – like water over a fierce fire that never boils
Or mountain snow that gives the sun brightness

13.

The drink-sodden Churchill won a war but he had to fight
    only his friends
For fifty years Balakirev wrote a piano sonata
It might have been done in an afternoon and worked on
    longer
Perhaps the wind waving the blade of grass in the scrub by
    the road draws the machine Leonardo would have
    invented if he'd lived a day longer
Its easy to understand
How I love you

14.

A holm oak grows by the hollow where the bomb fell on the
    edge of the field
And scattered earth on the grass like a mad sexton digging a
    grave though no one is dead
Shadows on the heavy grass stir like shadows on flesh
In the night a dew pond gathers
Cows stand at the rim and chew
Flanks twitch and tails whisk
Their hides shine like silk
An hour after dawn I sit with my feet stretched down the
    green slope
Over the pit a lark sings with the shrill voice of a child on the
    end of a diving-board
In the wood a pheasant croaks once
Always in many places the wind searches through litter and
    grass and curtains and washing drying on lines
A tin sheet flaps in a ruined barn – the roof has fallen in and
    the door leans on its frame – it is open to sun and rain

15.
How do you look now ?
Your hair is the colour of violin strings
Your face is scarred by the knifeblows friends strike from
    within
Or fragile with time ?
Do you hide it in paint ?
Perhaps your eyes rest on things with security ?
And your mouth is shaped by telling the truth for years
And the lines on your face hold the skin like stained glass in
    the light

I dont know where you live
Sometimes in strange cities I park at the curb and wait
Or walk the streets for an hour
I would know you
As I spoke I would see in your eyes the astonishment I saw
    in them when you first knew how I loved you
Would we drink tea ?
Get out our diaries ?
Go to bed ?
For a while be as we were – paper that holds the shape of the
    present it once held

16.
Perhaps you are dead ?
Stepped quickly from the pavement without looking
And for the last minutes of your life lay in the street
I hope someone cradled your head and lent you a jacket
And told you you werent dying
And crushed your lifeless hand with a grip as strong as a vice
    in a vice
So that you said: Whatsoever I feel of my strength, that I live
And died certain of living
What became of your body wouldnt bother me
Not interested in plots and shrines
Or reading wills
All I have is from you

17.
The life of orderly work
I eat at a round table
I work at an oblong desk on which lie my appointment book
    and patients' records
On my shelves medical dictionaries and specialists' reports
I drive to conferences
I talk with the sick
I learn
I see the number of those younger than me grows so that the
    world is kept well and strong
And you ?
You were so courteous when you branded me that it made
    me courteous
You showed me how to handle all things with care
Because they are yours
And all that I have is yours though you will never use it
I keep it for one who will not come
Perhaps I will forget you soon
Is that how it ends ?
Lie in bed and not think of you

18.
Near the end of surgery
A small green pill-bottle on the edge of my desk
Sunlight on the shoulder shaped like a segment of globe
An old woman sits hunched before me
Maroon felt hat
Hairs over lip
Under her eyes patches as delicate as the lines of thumb
    prints
She lives alone
Perhaps she sees people as strange – as an animal might see
    them
She looks at me calmly

Some diseases are caught by cringing before time
Shielding your eyes may blind you
Walking away may cripple you
You may break your back as you lift your burden to place it
    on another's shoulders
And an arrow shot long ago before wars were recorded may
    circle the earth till this morning it enters a child's head as
    it suddenly looks up from its play and it may be brought to
    die on your surgery floor
When the scythe is sharp and the reapers are tired they rest
    by sharpening the scythe – what else ?

Soon the woman will stand and walk back to her flat
The questions asked in this room are also asked in shops and
    factories and schools
Whispered face to face in kitchens and shouted above the
    crowd
The lovers' murmurs are the cries of the city muffled in night

19.
You could have had the apple
To get it you only had to cut down the tree
I would have joyfully pulled down the world
Sat in the wreckage and chewed my apple
Yes sat in the broken branches and munched like a spider
And eaten when trees grew in the ruins
But the faces of others – their broken bodies
Must be mended
Or I cant love you
That is why I love you
Lovers seek themselves and find others
And stand chaste in the naked crowd

20.
Car door on the parking lot
My wife
Our daughter's for dinner
The receptionist has been in buttoning her cardigan to tell
    me the waiting room is empty
I have completed the old woman's card
In the corridor red chrysanthemums on the windowsill
Lions' heads of tongues
I take them from the vase and shake the water from the
    stems

Orpheus and the Wire

Part Songs for Chorus

1.
Poets have sung of Orpheus
Who returned from hell
In this century day after day
Many go to hell in war or prison
Or walk there through the streets
And return home in the evening
Like Orpheus without his passion
Of them let Orpheus sing

2.
It was not permitted
That Orpheus and Eurydice
Rode in the same railtruck
Both mounted the ramp
But at different times
They last saw each other
Over a frozen wave of wire
Perhaps their ashes mingled
The point to note is this
When Eurydice was killed
They killed Orpheus

3.
After the war a philosopher said
In this hell let no poet speak
Orpheus be silent !

But Orpheus has always sung in hell
At night dreamed he led Eurydice through the barbed wire
And in the morning woke
And fought his enemies

And didnt the prisoner cut his vow deep in the wall ?
The tired worker study his master's skills ?
And the housemaid admire the cleanliness of the step
Her mistress saw only when she'd fouled it with her boots ?

4.
There was music before men and women
Before creatures grunted and called
The sea and wind sounded
Trees rattled on mountain-drums
Stones thundered on rocks
Volcanoes roared
And ice cracked

Restless and ceaseless
With the first light there was music
And later men and women came to sing songs
And sometimes they sing in the streets
The terrible songs of truth

5.
What's left at the master's table
Is taken out to the beggars' door
One hour a week the master's tutor
Instructs the beggar-children
Then returns to sleep in his master's house
At christenings the priest brands the beggar-children
With his master's mark
And god gives mercy to all

These gifts must be rejected
Or you go hungry for food and knowledge
And most of all mercy must be rejected
For god offers mercy to the master

6.
What was hell like ?
I'd never seen such a place
Music sounded like silence
(That is hard to imagine ?)

What was it like ?
No echo came from my music
Wind stole it and took it away
I dont know where it took it
For the first time I walked in silence
The ground lay under soft ash

It was an empty street
A secret policeman watched from a window

7.
A miser dropped a coin into a drain
A man passing
Helped him lift the iron grate
The miser climbed into the drain
And came back with his coin

The man said
While you were in the drain
I peered in to see that you were safe
A coin fell from my pocket into the drain
Go down again or hold the grate
So I may go down

The miser would not
And went away with his coin
And perhaps if Orpheus had brought
Eurydice from hell
The people would have done well
To stone him

8.
That jealousy took Orpheus to hell
Should also be considered
And it is certain that the goat
Feeding on grass by the gate
Did not stop chewing when Orpheus passed
Or even look up

9.
By the Styx I stoop
To pick from the muddy bank
A piece of broken crockery
On which are painted
Three blue flowers

So before hell was built
There was a city here
And perhaps people came to this river
To picnic

10.
I stood in the Styx
Icy water round my ankles
The dog stank and the ferryman
Who'd taken so many people to the ovens
Fussed over his duckboards
Water dripped from his oars
Like saliva from hungry mouths
At the stench of charred flesh

The judges counted lists of numbers
The law books were used to prop open
The doors of their shacks
It was the quiet time of day
Towards evening
After the battles and before the raids
When only the old and sick and suicides die

An hour ago I played my lute
No one listened
The ferryman doesnt even hear his own farts

My music is for comrades and friends
My enemies dont know how to hear music
The orchestra dies in their head

11.
Pressed by the weight of the world
By others' burdens we have not shared
With sorrow for friends who sold out to the enemy
Of dead heroes and heroines
Of strangers we have not warned
I wish for the still music of Orpheus

And at news too
Of a dictator dead in America
That somewhere the starving have taken bread
From those who argue the morality of rifles
In cities guarded by rockets
And at a flag that flutters in breeze
Where no poor shiver in rags
Then I hear the songs of Orpheus
Which are the songs of the free in prison

12.
Old now
More strings on this lyre than hairs on my head
I sit in the grass and lean on a tree
I look down at the river
All shadows have left the water
It shines like a fish's scales

Passing from childhood to youth was difficult
I needed the surgeon's knife
And her ?
That passion is gentle now
Seen through the open doorway
Beyond the pain
Where the sun shines gently on fields

And there is still music
At first it was wild
Earth sang in my throat
Later all my notes came from my fingertips
People still come to my door
For songs at weddings and births
And at buryings
Now my music has changed for the last time
I sing with the earth a cappella

My music didnt tame beasts
I dont know why men tell such rumours and lies
My music is simple
I strike three notes !
That heron – a broken stick – looks once
Then goes back to its fishing
But it is true that I went to hell
And like you I lost Eurydice

13.
Apollo gave Orpheus a lyre
On which to sing Apollo's hymns
And made Orpheus his instrument
Till in time beauty became cruel
And music was played at the poisoner's feast
Then the tractor destroyed the wooden plough
And Orpheus broke Apollo's lyre
The world was filled with new music
New dancers
And Apollo lay dead in the silence
Of hell

14.
When the slave sits in a corner
And polishes the links of his chain
I do not despair
At my friend's servility
His chain wont reach to the door
And his work shows only
His love of brightness

15.
I look at my hands
I dont know how they work
Or how music is made
I studied music
But it is still something
Given to me by others

And now I am old I think
It was never my music
It was Eurydice's voice
The voices of all in hell

And it is not strange
That this music calms me
There are still fools in power
But I have seen fools lose power
And learned how they lose it
And this created my craft
And therefore I praise this world
In music

A Prince Goes to his Wedding

A Prince Goes to his Wedding

Horses pull the carriage over the lines
Painted to guide lorries and cars
They're burying the dead in Ireland
The shopkeeper's daughter's on a bomb-buying spree
Half the world's red
I cant remember how many children are starving
(Where do the parents get the strength to beget 'em ? –
A sense of humour helps in my situation)
The bells make it hard to think
So many things mixed up topsy-turvy
I pass between rows of subjects
That remind me of faces behind camp wire
But these faces are cheering
Why do I think of such nasties
On this jolly day of rejoicing ?
Somewhere in the crowd there might be a pistol
Wrapped in a bit of bunting
I've stolen a day from the past
From the time of good old Queen Vicky
And she died – o humbldy-dumbldy centuries ago !
That's why this is a fool's day
Everything in it is dead

Hell

Many who could enter paradise tonight will sleep in hell
The owners of cinders are proud
The rakers of cinders are humble
The counters of cinders are blind
The trickster pitches his sale on your doorstep
In democracy all are free !
He gives you an urn and a rake
And sends you off to the ash heap
The cinders are warm as flesh

Today in the newspaper:
Four rapes in the city
An ascetic sells celibacy
In Lima starving loot food trucks
In Ireland a hunger strike
In the business centre a retiring banker shares his lifetime's
    experience: all men are crooks
How shall we know ourselves ?
Know the world and what you do in it
Then you will know who you are and what you should do
But you say 'In paradise we will weep when dust gets in our
    eyes'
And so tonight
We sleep in hell

Terror

The shopkeeper's daughter said
We will not give in to terror
Terrorism is not politics
Terrorists are criminals
I will protect our way of life

The shopkeeper's daughter said
To protect our way of life
I will unleash on my enemies
Such terror the earth has not seen
In all the annals of war and crime

These contradictions show
The end of a way of life
When for a time terrorists
In the place of government
Hold their nation hostage

A Little Poem With Many Brackets

It occurs to me
Watching TV and reading the press
That as the prince rode to his wedding
Amid the ringing of bells
(The sighing of jobless)
(The groaning of bankrupts)
(The thigh-slapping of bankers)
(The lip-smacking of bailiffs)
(The back-clapping of murderers)
(The hand-shaking of ministers)
(The whispering of spies)
(The clanking of guns)
(The clinking of medals)
(The creaking of crutches)
(The collapsing of houses)
(The burning of shopping centres)
(The rustling of court-rooms)
(The slopping-out of prisons)
(The stench of bunkers)
(The scent of wreaths)
(The hammering of nails into lids)
(The revving of hearses)
(The silence of the dead)
He might chalk up on the side of his carriage
(Not the number of H-bombs he will inherit – but)
The number
(I have used many brackets so that history may be
    understood)
Of hunger strikers
(Hey-nonny-nonny-no of the wedding we sing !
When the rose is plucked the thorn doesnt wither
And winter cant know the young joys of spring)
Who died in the nuptial year

The Incident

1. The Swing

At the circus where five roads meet
Before breakfast a soldier stood with a rifle
And looked down one of the streets
In the distance a child of five on a swing in a doorway
Shooting out from the side of the house like a cuckoo in a
    clock
Her socks crumpled down on her stiff legs

Perhaps a mother who didn't want her child to play in the
    street in these troubled times
Had hung a swing from two hooks in the lintel of her front
    door
So that she could say to the child
When the swing goes forward you're in the street !

A passer-by said to the soldier who stood with his rifle where
    five roads meet
This morning at least someone is happy !
He said
The little bastard's been told to keep her eye on me

2. Questions

Sergeant last night the street was dark
The pools of light by the street-lamps were full of shadows
I shot the man
But was he running away from me when I shot him
Or reeling with drink ?

Soldier you ask who the man was
Where did he work ?
Did he sit alone in the evenings
Or drink with those he respected and loved ?

Useless questions !
Ask did you shoot him before he shot you ?
The dead are terrorists
Its not your job to explain what the dead were up to

3. The Puddle

In the bright early morning
A woman returning from night work
Saw blood on the pavement
Bent to look
The top of her head appeared in the puddle
Quickly she turned and went home

She had passed her son's blood on the pavement
Strange !
Yet those who build the street poured so much concrete and
    followed so many orders that their blood is on every stone
The city is kept alive with their blood
Even while they go on their business their bodies lie under
    the streets like foundations
Yet the streets are not named after them – they are not
    permitted to say our factory – or we built this city for
    ourselves and our children
Nor are they asked what they think till its too late to solve
    the problem by thinking
Each day the woman passes her children's blood on the
    street without seeing
And no one points to it for her
Really that is much stranger !

There is not one god and one enemy
Or one nation and one mother
Each life and each death is different
In this world the laws are upside down
The red moon shines on the pavement

4. *The Search*

The woman slept in her house
Soldiers knocked and she opened her door
Her world turned upside down
The soldiers entered their house and searched for their things
They tagged their books and their clothes with their numbers
They read their letters and stared at their photos
She sat on their kitchen chair with her hands on their table
If they had handcuffed her hands they would have been their
    hands
She was a trespasser in their house
A fugitive in the foreigners' city

5. *The Jacket*

My son was to be best man
I sent his jacket to the cleaners
So that he'd look good

At the lads' party the night before he'd had a few jars
Coming home he dropped his jacket when the soldiers
    shouted
They ran over it with their boots
It was dirty before they shot him

Now I've sent his jacket to the cleaners
So it looks good on him in the box

6. The Grip

When terrorists bomb the city
Lynch law stirs in the judges' hearts
And the city may go in fear of judges and bombs
But when the prison bars are broken each morning
The gaoler cannot repair them and loses his prisoners

The English held Ireland so long their claws rooted
Not that the grip was alive and adapted to each of the
    victim's shudders and twists
But that the grip of the dead is harder to break

The Demonstration

They Never Learn

After the war of the little racist
When fifty millions lay dead
And more gentiles than jews had been killed
It was said now they will learn

Yet here are the racists parading with beating drums
To tell us no jews were killed
And that the Auschwitz smoke is a lie
They cant tell us no gentiles were killed
Our fathers were killed

So we fight
Or they will go on adding dead to dead
Because they never learn
And we always forget

The March

Parading beside the left-wing march
Eight young men in the strength of youth
Spin to face the marchers as if in a dance
And raise their arm in the stiff salute
Sieg heil !

After fifty years of silence and screams
While they ticked their grubby lists
Will we see them grey and respectable
Quietly walking beside their wife in the park ?

Each day in the street we pass monsters
We do not see them
Nor do we see their victims
More than we fear the monsters
We should fear the victims
And be shocked less by the shouts
Than the silence

The Killing

Twice before the blows that killed him he was beaten
By fascists in the war against reason
After these attacks those sworn to destroy the law
Left him wounded in the street
After the third attack those sworn to defend the law
Left him in the street to die

Many are killed in backrooms in quiet streets
Where no one can see the killing
And come forward to name the killer to the police
He was killed by police in front of police
Yet no one came forward to say what they had seen
And name the killer

So we wonder what use are police sworn to defend the law
And how shall we defend ourselves against the defenders of
   law who kill a man on the street ?

Praise

To all martyrs and makers of peace
Who in darkness kept the light
In time of folly reasoned
In famine did not sell their mouths or hands for bread
In turmoil desert their comrades
Or in defeat lose hope
We give a red carnation
And our word to keep the struggle

To all women and men who died
So that we could walk freely in streets through which they
   were led in chains or driven in sealed vans
To all who studied with disciplined minds to give strategy to
   the struggle
To all who lived in cells or died on the torturer's bench so
   that our children should play in joy
We give a red carnation
And our word that their struggle is our struggle
For we are the many who cannot fail in the fight of the
   martyrs and makers of peace

London Ballads

I
The old man wanders from suburb to suburb
Blowing a horn
Felt hat the colour of late evening sky
A long white beard stained at the edges by rain
A bundle rolled in green canvas tied with a cord
A shirt a damp towel a bit of soap
And an old Gillette razor
He sharpens the blade on the curb
No buttons missing from the mac
On a string he leads a black labrador
When he washes or sleeps he ties the string to his ankle
He and the dog are never untied
They eat and shit on the string
The dog stares at the world
And tries to understand
Its expression cannot change anymore
They say the man looks for a lost woman
Calling her on the horn
  But he accepts pennies

II
Black pillars of smoke spiral into the sky
And slink along under the clouds like crooks searching for a
  way of escape
At night smoke lingers higher up before the stars
A thin veil from wars blown round the world
A sudden wind yelps on a corner
A mother calls her child
Rain begins to fall down the window panes
The house is weeping
First you see faces
  Then you see how many backs there are in the city

III

Peabody Buildings
Nineteenth-century philanthropist's tenements
Grey stones and cream sills and mullions
Before the flats were modernised there were communal sinks
    on the landings
A window at street level is usually open
In it a woman sits wrapped in woollies and cardigans
She is blind
She stirs her tea in a cup on the ledge
The bowl of the spoon is shaped like an eye
It flashes in and out of the brown whirlpool
    She sits like a question

IV

Londoners live in other people's houses
Who died a lifetime ago in this bedroom ?
Who came out on this landing to open a letter ?
What bride swept this floor on the first morning her husband
    left her for work ?
New houses on old bomb sites or sites cleared for profit
Sometimes it seems as if in this bustle
The dead moved in the graveyard and the stones swayed
So many privet hedges
So many curtains stained by fingers
So much groaning and laughter in chimneys
So many warnings pushed through letterboxes and threats
    banged on walls
So many shadows that stand still in doorways while the sun
    moves
It is a listening city
    And says live here – it is good – in the bricks by the
        river

Going to Work

1. Graffiti

On the abandoned factory wall
Bring Back the Rope
Wogs Out
As if a giant had bitten the bricks and scraped them with its
　　teeth

2. Butcher

Butcher face to face with his customer over the marble slab
In one hand a hatchet – the other rests on the till
Apron of prison bars – boater stolen from manger
Never was a butcher who didnt smile at his customer and
　　offer lean cuts in the house of offal
She goes off feather nodding on hat

3. Old People's Garden

Weary weary said the snail weary I travel
I screw my body into my shell as if my flesh hung from a
　　hook in my head
If the crow cracked my walls they would be grist for his crop
　　when he ate me
On the path the silver trail of ghost's blood
A snail living under the feet of the mob

4. White Face

The whiteness – the coldness – of snow passes
Runs into rivers – the rivers are large
Lonely confusion – despair – the white face remains
Only one spring – one harvest – one season of understanding
When the winds that shook the trees are gone
The face white as snow – remains
As if new bandages were tied on the wounds of the dead

5. Soldier on a Train

Little whey-faced soldier thin as a child
Holding your fag like an expert
Your collar is loose and you wear your boots as if they were
    in their box
Are the enemy animals to be hunted because they wear
    camouflage-gear and yip in terror ?
And what of the white-faced woman helping the white-haired
    grandmother out of bed in the raid ?
And the man hurrying to reach his house – the key sent
    flying onto the path next door ?
You were happy at home with your people
In afternoons when the house was crowded with empty rage
    you could have walked in the street – it wasnt no man's
    land
Or gone into your neighbours – the door wasnt booby-
    trapped
Was killing the good life ?
The army trained you with a lie: they told you you are brave
Whey-faced soldier they didnt tell you soldiers are afraid
And kill when they shit themselves like children

6. *The Tyrant Sat on a Hill*

The tyrant sat on a hill over the battle
Too high to count dead soldiers or kiltering guns or hear
    horses' screams
Dust rose and his eyes ran
The staff whispered among themselves: such charity
Later state funerals
He threw a handful of dust in the great grave
The wind had not fallen
His reputation rose even higher

7. *The Hawk in the Air*

The hawk in the air !
It passes ! – it passes ! – and leaves no trace
The eyes are dry when the last tear runs down the face and
    soon the mourners sleep
The world is merciful
But ask: when the monster was built in my city
Did I offer my skin for the mass-graft to cover the frame ?
Give my blood when the arteries were inaugurated ?
Register at the counter when they asked for brains to tip into
    its dustbin skull ?
And take the stone from my shoe so that I could walk round
    the mountain ?
Or did I join the conspiracy before the monster could send
    the young people to die ?
Run messages ? Shelter the assassins ? Hide the gun in my
    mac ?
Shout louder than the orders ? Question the instructions ?
    Interrogate the torturers ?
I have thrown roses on ash heaps in death camps
But the murderers still parade in our streets
In filthy sweatshirts or with polished holsters and straps
Why am I not angry at the horrors of peace ?

8. Some Die Alone in Gutters

Some die alone in gutters
They are not mourned
Police take them away and attach a number in lieu of a name
They do not ask what good came from their lives but the
  cause of death
Always searching and prying and burying truth under forms
  they discard on the floor
Mice devouring old photos in derelict houses
When a wolf dies each wolf – even the cubs – sniffs it before
  the pack goes on
Strangers sniff these dead and mark the file social derelict –
  foul play not suspected
Yet as legacy they leave us the cause of their death
And if we dont name the culprits we inherit the crime

9. In Autumn Birds Fly South

In autumn birds fly south
When the leaves have fallen more birds are seen in the forest
Some of them worry at this sudden invasion
Where shall we turn at the crossroads ?
Is that the horizon or the lip of the abyss ?
Are we meeting or parting ?
Crowds rush like clouds in a storm
So fast they leave their band behind them
Playing alone in the desert

10. A Magpie Flying Over Water

The magpie by the ambitious lake calls its messages
The murderer turns away as he strikes lest the corpse
    identify him
When the worm wriggles it thinks its fighting the hook
The nest needs only one leaf for shelter – let the bird build at
    the first sign of spring
When the bread attacks the knife the bread must win

11. Paradise is a Place of Plenty

Paradise is a place of plenty where there is no evil
They say the gods drove it away
We are not gods
If we would live happily we must take power from evil
But evil is armed
The evil do not listen to reason – that is why they are evil
The evil are not moved by tears – the crying of the evil is the
    laughter of the good – they howl and tears run on their
    face
Not even the gods could destroy evil
They drove it out but keep a guard on the door
And we are not gods
You do not disarm evil by lowering your head to the block

12. The Pine

Year after year the pine grows to the moon
It would take time to talk to the murderers and it would be
    wasted
You might as well set out to melt the polar ice with a box of
    matches

13. Harsh Frost

Harsh frost – mouth cant smile
Wind blows all expression from face
Under the coiled rope – the anchor

14. One Day a Man Made the First Cage

One day a man made the first cage
He was pleased with his useful thing
In it he shut a wolf
One day he made the first spear
He threw it at a tiger
It sang in the air and quivered with laughter as it stuck in
    the tiger's flank
The man shouted with joy – a new coat! – warm ! –
    splendid !
He used the spear gash as the mouth of a pocket
One day he made the first cup and carried water to the old
    and sick
Nor did he learn to speak so that he could threaten and lie
But one day to add to his possessions he made the first slave
The slave crouched in a back alley weary with labour
The alley was silent – the whole sky came to stare at him
And from that day men started to make their cities cages and
    throw spears at each other
Now only the slave can save them from the life of the tiger
    and the death of the wolf

15. It Would be Better if Birds Did Not Sing in Cages

It would be better if birds did not sing in cages
But pined and died in an hour
The world sings to us as if we were emperors on our way to
   the games
There are trumpets even in the poor parts of the city !
Never make music for emperors – they have the arena roar
It would be better for us when we picked fruit if the tree
   asked who was hungry
It would be better for us when we took up stones if they told
   us whose blood was already on them
It would be better for us when we built a wall if the bricks
   told us the slogans they would have to bear
It would be better for us if birds did not sing in cages

16. A Gift

In a tree on a sidewalk two branches hold out a bunch of
   flowers
No one took them so they withered
A common sort of tree and both ends of the street are much
   the same
I look closer and see the flowers are a few leaves left on the
   tree in winter
Carry your burdens: they will provide for the journey
If there are too many obstacles the road disappears but you
   can build a new one
The heap of rubble would make a look-out for you to see
   where you're going
But you must take the gifts that are offered

17. When a Great Building

When a great building in which many have passed their lives
Is demolished
There is an explosion
A groan that echoes inside itself with a deep sigh
And for a while wraiths of dust drift where the building stood
When a tree falls there is no explosion
The chainsaw stops
Silence – slowly the trunk leans – a creak like an unoiled
    hinge
Then a hushed clatter as branches and twigs take the force of
    the fall and ease the trunk to the ground
As if it were lowered by children's hands
A sound made before we were on the earth
Yet it is like a human death – the earth is torn and light goes
    from the branches

18. She Died

She died
I tidied her room and picked up a tissue she'd dropped on
    the floor
We dress the dead and fasten their buttons as if they were
    children
And often the old live in the child's world – their days are
    numbered in meals and they go to bed early
A gateway stands at each end of the long room
The young call to the old to play with them in their gateway
And when the rain fell I saw them flatten themselves to the
    wall
And the young run to bury their face in their side

19. Dear Friend

Dear friend because you lived so long and died with such
    modesty
We shall recover and do not have to live with the wounds
    that killed you
How carefully you folded your napkin after you'd eaten as
    sparingly as a tree eating its own fruit
You slept little – lay with eyes as wide as a shore that knows
    the tide will return
You knew that Troy had fallen but not the colour of
    Agamemnon's scarf – which is not knowledge
You knew the old peasant woman had died but not how
    many plates she'd brought in her dowry – though that
    would have told you much about her life
You liked your grandchildren to be dressed brightly
You spoke little and your unstressed words had the candour
    of engineer's drawings
And once you saw snow fall in the southern sea
We mourn for the happiness we lost with you
But you still give us gifts if we take them

20. Rain

Rain on the roof
A clown's drumroll or soldiers parading ?
Executioners practising ?
Condemned shaking the bars ?
Questioners tapping the windows ?
The feet of running children ?
Ticking before the explosions ?
A world's tears ?
All these things woke you

21. The Fire

Dogs snarl and nuzzle – bicker and romp
These contradictions keep the pack close and all goes well
Till no rain falls
The rivers parch – the rocks are as hot as ovens – the lizards
 rot
And one by one the whimpering dogs are silent and die

We are kind and angry and in this way we make a
 community
Kindness alone will not save us from the death of dogs
In the time of famine and plague and fire do not stamp out
 the fire but carry it to the plague-field to burn out the
 pestilence
Then dig a channel to bring water to govern the fire and
 grow crops against famine
Unless we take the fire to the plague-field we shall not live to
 bring water to the crop
And it is kinder to soak the smouldering ground and feed the
 famished than carry them to the river bed as cracked as
 their parched lips

22. Ant

On the rehearsal room floor an ant
I watch the actors
Buddhists drink tea through a mouth-cloth that would dress
 a wound or a doll
Perhaps the gut is the bug's paradise ?
Jump for joy and you squash a beetle
Kneel to thank god for his creatures and you flatten a spider
I remove the ant

23. *Partridges*

Green shoots no taller than stubble
From this distance buoys bobbing at sea
Seven partridges crossing a cornfield
If only actors spoke with the severe caprice of the partridges'
  bobs in the furrows
And they dont even know its the hunter's field

24. *Questions*

Ignorant teenagers !
After I talk they are silent and I ask questions !
How will they learn if they dont ask questions ?
At twelve we said at thirteen you're not a child !
These are children !

Or perhaps its what they already know that keeps them
  silent ?
Perhaps for a long time they've known things they dont tell
  in front of teachers ?
Perhaps things that astonished us are commonplaces to
  them ?
And the things before which their parents were silent will
  make them speak out ?

Good ! already they know much and will learn more
Now they are clever
Later they will ask questions

25. *Politeness*

Many deserve our scorn
And you can fall in love on a street corner
Animals have analogues of our passions
But politeness is human
It cant be learned from books of manners
It is the strategy of the desperate
Be polite to your enemies
Anger is dirt in the gunsights
When we live in a human world we wont kill each other
It wouldnt be polite

26. *Horse by the Road*

So long at the cart – now it grazes the verge
A wad of newspaper like a sodden bruise in the trod grass
Its nostrils are as sensitive as a child's hand – old gods would
    pray to be given such hands
Air fills the huge body like water in a stone trough
An old woman comes on the path to talk to it
Ground-pawer with hoofs like centuries
Be content and at peace
All is well

27. *Two Worlds*

The hands holding the child against me
Are in two worlds: the palms warm and the backs of the
    hands in the wind
Perhaps my two eyes dont look from the same head and one
    side of my mouth speaks against the other ?
If the ground rocks tell the child its a cradle
If the walls fall tell it they throw bricks for a game
If the earth opens at my feet – I dont know what I'll do
I'll find a way to get through

28. Leaves

All leaves whisper in one wind
No leaf speaks louder than another
Argument makes democracy strong
But you must listen carefully to hear each leaf when storms
  toss the trees

29. Early Morning

Spring sky – grime washed from the big window
On the streets and open spaces light falls as if they'd been
  unveiled this morning
On the neighbours' lawn stalks of grass bent at the angle of a
  child's head as it looks at the teacher

30. We Let It Happen

Light shines through the eyes onto the back of the skull
A film projector running in ruins
An insect's legs stick through a fissure
Why ? Why ? Why ?

31. Dust

The smell of dust
Not dust on things but from in things
From crushed plaster and broken bricks
Fallen walls – splintered wood – torn joists
After bombs slats grin in lopsided ceilings
Forty years yet still sometimes the air smells of dust
As if the wind blew it from new ruins
Or old ruins falling apart

Reports and Chronicles

Reports and Chronicles

Lau Tzu

Lau Tzu sat in a boat
Reading a book
Dust fell on the page

Later they said
What did you read ?

He said
On history

They said
While you read
An army marched passed on the shore
To conquer the northern kingdom
And drive the people before the slave whips
And bring the lord of the north to the capital
To cut off his head in front of the emperor's screen

The boat slowly nodded

He said
Yes but the officers do not know what history is
And forbid us to talk with those who do

Wu Qui

General Wu Qui wore the uniform
Of the common soldier
Ate the same rations
Carried his kit on his back in an issue knapsack
Marched with the ranks – his litter was used to carry the
    emperor's orders
At night slept on the ground
And when a soldier's wound got gangrene
Sucked out the pus

On hearing this the soldier's mother
Wailed

Her neighbours said
Woman ! your son is a common soldier
The general has sucked pus from his wound
Why do you wail ?

The mother answered
His father was also a soldier
When the gash in his leg turned septic
His excellency Wu Qui sucked out the pus
This made him too proud to retreat in battle
Or turn his back on the enemy
He was soon killed –
The woman wailed –
And now this calamity has struck our son !

The Anatomy of Learning

The anatomist Vesalius is showing his Brussels aunt
The sights of Padua
Marcantonio Cantari judge of the criminal court
Has delayed my execution to the end of her visit
When the learned doctor will be free
To demonstrate my cadaver before his students
Thus even the poor share the benefits of learning

The Beauty Mark

In china there was a girl who was so happy and knew such
    peace that not once since she came to this world had she
    smiled or cried
So that her face was flawless white
Till the day she shed one tear – she would not say for what –
That left where it fell on her cheek a purple mark
This brought her great fortune
The emperor married her

Later a customer – the wife of a middle-rank official –
Confessed to a woman who served at the counter of a
    leather-goods shop and knew about hides
That she longed to see the great beauty with the plum-
    coloured streak on her face
The woman replied as she wrapped her customer's purchase
That she could not see what would be gained by staring at a
    poor girl who not once since she came to this world had
    stopped crying

From the Fields Voices Call

From the fields voices call
The messenger has been sighted
The people run to the square of beaten earth before the
        citadel
The messenger rides his horse through the archway
His mouth is a straight line
Steam shoots from his horse's nostrils
What news ? What news ?
If the marquis' soldiers have won
The people will be given a portion of rice
The marquis will celebrate all night
Till the guttering oil-lamps make daylight dirty
How eagerly his household waited for the baggage train !
The marquis promised his daughter a carpet
The field marshal was instructed to choose a good one from
        the loot
But if the marquis' soldiers have lost
The veils of his women will be as if cut in stone
His children will be silent for weeks
And the people will not see their husbands and fathers and
        sons again
In these local wars no prisoners are taken
His servants say:
Break a cup today and he laughs – break it tomorrow – they
        strap you in with the mules that work the mill in the yard
All day the marquis will sit hunched before his collection of
        unusual pebbles
The servants will avoid meeting him in the corridors and
        neglect their duties
The hibiscus will wither in its earthenware pot
And later a frightened serving girl will be sent in to sweep up
        the fallen leaves
So that the marquis is not reminded of how his soldiers failed
        to give him his victory

Clay Figures

Egyptians made clay figures
Bakers with loaves – often one loaf was burned
Weavers binding grass bales
Sailors in ships from which no sea would wash the dust
Farmers bent at the plough in the potter's field
And toys for the offspring born to the dead in the afterlife
And put them in their tombs
Strange ways of the pharaohs !
If the dead had risen not even the burned loaf would have
    reconciled them to the world of clay
They would have killed themselves with the clay knife

In our world
Clay soldiers stand guard on the clay-fields
Laws are fired on bricks of clay
Clay pitchers are set by clay bread
We send our children to work in the clay ovens
At night they return with clay on their hands
The egyptians held funeral rites for the dead
We hold them for the living
Unveil on our streets iron heroes cast in clay moulds
And rifle the land like robbers come from the grave
Strange are our ways !
When we might throw on the potter's wheel
The clay from the sexton's spade

The Flood

I

Noah asked the dove what it had seen
The dove told of desolation in all the earth
Great log-jams of tables and chairs and doors
Bottles and clothes and carts
Household furniture and equipment from farms and factories
Forced together by currents into rafts as big as nations
In places there were mountains of debris
Whole cities – ports and warehouses – had erupted through
    the water like volcanoes

After the dove had visited the world a second time
It returned and said the water was sinking
Already it had withdrawn from the mountain-tops
And chairs and tables and carpets stood on them
As if giants had come there to live

II

So the water sank into the seas and rivers and the ark came
    to rest in the puddles
Noah looked at the debris of cities and men that stood round
    him on the hills
And made a fire of furniture
And led the beasts and birds from the ark and sacrificed all
    of them on the fire
As thanksgiving to his god
Also he sacrificed his family
From the babe born on water high over the mountains
To those who had walked on the earth with greyheads before
    Noah was born
He sacrificed all to his god and sang the Te Deum

III

When the flood rose many people took to the water in boats
   they found in ports and moorings
Their names are not known
During the flood they ate fish and floating vegetables and
   fruit
The water gave to them more freely than the fenced fields
   before the flood
And they collected rain in buckets and drank and washed
   themselves and their clothes
When the water receded they entered the land – the wind
   dried the hills in a week – and went into the fields and
   cities and multiplied
And the lice and mice and insects that had gone with them
   in the stolen boats bred
And from them the beasts of the earth and the fowls of the
   air evolved
And the children of the flood filled the earth and farmed the
   fields and worked in great industries and prospered
   mightily in all the land

On the Uselessness of Christianity

He went for the traders with a whip
Chased them through the gates cursing and scorning
Ran after them down the steps so that the sandals flew from
   their feet
Calling on them to change their hearts
To speak justice
Then ran back to the temple
And threw over the last of the stalls
The terrified sacristans watched from a corner

He next saw the traders as he looked down at them from the
　　cross
They shook their fingers and wagged their beards as they
　　chattered and laughed
Smoke from the offerings on their lips
The mouths of their pockets soiled with coins
A manager on the way from Yafo to Zarqa
Stopping over in Jerusalem for a few days
To check his warehouse stocks
Took bets – how long to die ?

The Camel

Steady footfall of an army
Gentle roll of a forest roof
Beside it the driver
The seat of his robe thick with grease and oasis mud
Carries a stick

On its back carpetbags
Heavy with brass and bales of cotton
Dung and rind in the footprints before it
And a grass straw

Which the wind blows onto the camel's back
The old man's grin deepens on its great mouth
It goes on

A fly buzzes from the dung and lights on the straw
The weight runs down the beast's body
Its eyes stay on the horizon
It goes on

A grain of sand left in the air years ago by a storm
Drops on the fly
It falls

The caravan is late
The driver kicks its groin
And beats its snout till it caves in

It lies at rest
Some of its burdens scattered about it
The others roped to its back
Tilts its two left feet in the air
And dies

I Sought

I sought
I blew the dust from books
The letters were lines of ants marching up and down a tower
The last line of the book
Led to
The first line of the book

I sought
In a room I found musical instruments
A harp as big as a mainsail
A piano with as many keys as a city has windows
A trumpet with a mouth as big as a six-lane highway
The instruments were too big for music-making

I sought
I stood in a doorway at night
To follow the sages as they went to their secret meetings
Only drunks passed
Singing songs backwards

I sought
I heard a door bang in a suburban street
I saw a frightened mother in casualty reception
I saw workers hurrying to the factory carpark
I saw an old man on an iron railway bridge
And the books of wisdom fell open
And the necklace broke and the beads scattered
And the ground wore them in a new order

The Slave

He stands to be whipped
His skin is tough but it suffers
He tells himself it does not suffer
His glazed eyes – overwork – see the whip
He tells himself he does not see the whip
His face bows to his own shadow on the ground
By chance as the whip falls the weals on his back resemble –
    near enough – the letters
S L A V E
But he cannot read what is on his back

After the feast the owner throws crumbs to the floor
By chance they fall into the letters – near enough –
T H E F T
Hunger forces him onto all fours to eat the crumbs before he
    can read them

He stands before his killer
As the raised knife comes down
He sees in the bright blade his own
FACE
But he does not believe the blow is meant for him
Why should the master kill the loyal servant ?

When they blast you from your grave the dust of your bones
    will blind you !
The roar of their bombs will deafen you !
When will you see what you see and hear what you hear ?
When the crowd lifts its head to look at the master
The crowd has too many eyes to be blind
Then you will lift your fist
And it will be the fist of a crowd

Bertl Laux – Two Stories of a German Nurse

I

I was born long ago in the last century
My father forbade me to be a nurse
He loved me and wanted to shield me from pain
He has been dead for seventy years – can you believe it ?

I ran away to America to work as a lady secretary
When I had saved enough money
I came back to Europe
And paid for my medical studies in Switzerland

On the day I learned I had passed my examinations
Friends took me by steamer to Heligoland to celebrate
We drank wine in a café
The little iced cakes had silver patchouli on top
We were eating works of art I can tell you !
I suppose we were a bit noisy
And the day was long and sunny

When it was time to go
We stood on the quayside
I remember the people so well
We ladies wore long white dresses
And carried white sunshades with frills

Behind me stood an old man in a silk hat
And frock coat – that's what you English call them
(In those days gentlemen wore suits even on holiday)
There was a gold chain on his stomach
And a gold knob on his stick
And his spectacle frames were gold
He had a long white beard and big white side whiskers
And he was old – O old! – very old

It was towards evening
There was still hazy sunlight on the quay
I was young and my life was before me
And I had passed my examinations
So I clapped my hands and said
Now all I need is a war to show what a good nurse I am

The old man tapped my shoulder and said
Young lady you dont know what you say
We giggled

When the ferry reached Germany
The reflections of the quayside lamps bobbed in the water
In the streets there were hundreds of placards
The newspaper boys were shouting
Crown Prince shot at Sarajevo !

II
The entrance of the château near Brussels
Was like the porch of a Grand Hotel
Our ward had been the picture gallery
Through the great windows along the wall we saw the park
The light was good for our work

We were straightening beds and preparing patients
For the doctor's evening rounds
And the young soldier died
There was no time to take away his body
Or even close his eyes
The oak door opened and the doctor entered

The doctor was not a young man
Whose hands would tremble when he was tired
Or an old man who had fought many wars and learned how
    to shout at people in pain
To help them to be still
He was middle-aged – grey had just touched the side of his
    temples
And each morning he inspected his boots to make sure his
    batman had polished them

He stopped by the dead soldier and said
Open your mouth
The soldier's face was like ice under thin snow
I lifted my hand to speak
The cuff was starched white

The soldier will speak for himself !
Soldier I give you a military order !
This is dumb insolence !
Open your mouth !
I could have you shot !

Refugees

Each morning they read the newspapers
Listened to the radio
The streets were filled with flags
They billowed like flames from the windows and roofs

Small pennants fluttered in tired children's hands
As if the fire was spreading to them
Officials broadcast frenzied ravings with cold politeness
People lived to the beating of drums
The world was a burning ballroom

The man and woman gathered with their children in the hall
They kissed
She took the children to wait in the car
He stayed in the house to switch off the water and electricity
And destroy the family dog

They drove to the airport
The passport official half smiled
The stewardess betrayed only slight nausea
They had got away
For days they knew peace

A Story

From Germany at the uprising of Hitler
A jewess and her daughter came
To the island defended by sea

The news got darker
From their window on the horizon
They watched the shadow spread over Europe
Each morning when night withdrew
The shadow over the day was longer

So the mother went to the corner chemist
And pointed to two bottles of aspirin
At home she sat in the window with her daughter
Outside in the grey spring a blackbird dug for worms
When the fledglings flew
A sombre voice on the radio announced the fall of France

Each swallowed the aspirin from one bottle
The mother being worn died
The daughter lived
The doctor called it a miracle
What use is a miracle ?

She pleaded guilty to killing her mother
The law deals in generalisations
It demanded death
The judge whispered the sentence
So that the daughter would not hear it
And raising his voice said
I recommend the minister to grant a quick pardon
After six months the daughter was freed
To return to the flat where her mother had died

Here was a judge ashamed of the law he administered
So that he spoke it with lowered voice
But he was not a good judge
Each day he passed over in silence
Things he should have shouted from the roof of his court
The padre who like a valet dressed him in the hanging cap
That night ate his supper with this grace –
God hears the small voice in the storm

God we serve well
We whisper so he may choose to hear or not
It would be better to raise our voice over the storm
So that the city heard our shout for justice

The Sacrifice

Her pinched face had two expressions
Obstinacy and satisfaction
If her obstinacy drove you to drown her
Her last expression would be satisfaction

That she had proved you were evil
Everything her enemies did was wrong
If they built they destroyed the view
If they didnt build they were backward
She spoke to waiters like the mistress of a mansion
But now they didnt recognise the tone
So they were not offended
And served her as well as they did the others
Years ago her family had left their villas and parks and
    woods
At dawn with three suitcases
(I dont know what was in them)
And because their enemies could not catch them
They had drowned her dog in the sea
Now with the satisfaction that comes
From not listening to answers
She asked why ?
And could not understand what had been done to people
To make them throw a dog over a cliff
For they were the golden times
When the gardens were tended
And the house swept each morning
And at night guests for the hunting party sat on the terraces
To hear the farm workers sing
The songs they made from the hardness of their lives
She was intelligent and kindly
And often helped others
But she was never able to understand
Why one morning she and her family
Had run to the station with three suitcases
Or that she had tied a stone to the dog's neck
Before it was thrown from the terrace into the sea
Or that each day she venerated
The golden idol to which she had been sacrificed

The Stone

After a year the hill had changed
The stone had worn a groove and pushed earth from the top
    of the hill to the bottom
And Sisyphus rolled it on a level track
The next year as he walked he engineered rubble into a
    series of small hollows and rises
The momentum the stone gained in descending one rise took
    it close to the top of the next
So that he had to push it only the little way left to the top
And now while he worked he had time to study geology
    geography and soldiers
The annual report was sent to the ruler
He issued an order
Under escort Sisyphus rolled the stone over the province to
    the foot of a great mountain
The granite sides were steep and craggy
The new hardships made the work easier: the granite wore
    the stone till it was smoother and smaller
The soldiers were lazy (as soldiers are) and often lagged
    behind
Why should they work properly ?
Many times they came round a corner and found Sisyphus
    gazing ahead as he sat on the stone
When they wearied of following him they let him travel
    ahead for days on his own
He used these times to build a stone hut under a sheltering
    cliff close to the summit
Later he furnished it with tables and benches of stone and
    made a walled garden
Often the soldiers sat in his garden and talked of the
    lowlands
By now dust from the stone and the mountain had got into
    his skin so that he looked as if he had been carved of stone
Then there was the first accident
As it rolled down the slope the stone jumped over a dip and
    a third of it broke off
A year later the second accident happened

The stone crushed a soldier's foot
He could not march
The army decided he had been made unfit for duty by his
     own negligence
He was discharged without pension
The other soldiers demolished Sisyphus' hut and beat him
But not hard enough to get rid of their anger at the wrong
     done to their comrade and the miseries of their bad
     posting
If they had crippled him he could not have pushed the stone
     and then they would have been beaten
Their's was a hard life
In future they kept away from the stoneman
A year later – the third accident
The stone ran into the side of a herdsman's hut and knocked
     over his table as he and his family sat round it at dinner
By now the soldiers were a known menace
There had been rapes and brawls and robberies (as there are
     with soldiers)
So the herdsmen and farmers who lived on the mountain
     ambushed them in a defile and rolled boulders down on
     them from the cliffs
The soldiers made punitive raids on the villages
The villagers climbed higher into the mountains and lived in
     their ancestors' caves and used their paths
And made war on the soldiers as if they cut tombs for them
     in the living rock
Unwilling to fight the unequal battle the soldiers withdrew to
     their base in the foothills
But by then Sisyphus had long ago finished his labour and
     the stone was lost
This is the true story of Sisyphus which those who rule have
     been at pains to suppress

Ndzansk

On the coast a fortress
No port
The sea freezes for nine months of the year
The hinterland is a cordon of forests as deep as a continent
The town's main street was flagged and the side-streets mud
Houses and shops and civic buildings rose straight from the
    steep rock
Light falls evenly everywhere and rises again from the sea
Three centuries ago prisoners dug cells in the rock
And from the rock they dug out they built walls and
    gateways and offices over the cells
And then they were locked in the cells till they died
Each month an escorted herd of two-footed cattle
Staggered and slipped in chains up the steep streets to the
    gates in the rock walls
The butcher leaned in his doorway and the haberdasher
    looked up from his counter
Both lived from the herds who bought nothing: the guards
    and their families bought
The cattle passed through the gateway into the holes in the
    rock
All sentenced for life
One in a cell – a dead chrysalis
No light
When a door was locked it was not opened till the bones
    were thrown in the sea
Sometimes an engineer sealed a feed-hole with iron
The order took three months to reach him – the job thirty
    minutes
Sometimes a prisoner beat open his head on the wall
Or tried to starve
After three weeks he crouched on the floor in delirium
And caught food in his mouth as it fell from the hole
His madness made his life-sentence longer by adding new
    miseries
On duty the soldiers functioned like machines
They didnt talk to the prisoners or to each other

In the opera house operas were played to an audience in red
  tunics and evening dress a year after the première in
  Bruxelles or Paris
There was a lending library
A society for antiquarians
Another to catalogue creatures and plants of the forest and
  sea
And another to study rocks
The town had a joke: if a prisoner dug through the rock
  when the sea was frozen he could run to America
In the thaw the sea struck the rock and the cells trembled
In the gales even the prisoners' limbs shook
When the monthly herds grew larger
The new prisoners were sent to fell pines in the forest
The ground shook as the trees crashed in a wreckage of
  timber and light
Prisoners yoked to the trunks dragged them back to the
  fortress
Between the outer walls and the offices they built a
  dormitory barracks
And then cut new cells in the rock
As they dug the blows of the sea and their sledge-hammers
  made the rock tremble
And now when the new prisoners fed the old prisoners there
  was a smell of pine as if the rock ran with sap
More soldiers were posted to the fortress
They walked beside their wives to the butcher and
  haberdasher
And prosperity came to the town
Membership of the library and learned societies grew
It was forbidden to display metropolitan papers in the public
  reading-room
And the prisoners' barracks were burned three times
And three times the prisoners and soldiers shot at each other
Before the governor was lowered on a rope down the side of
  the wall and swung like a pendulum till he stopped
And the shops of the butcher and haberdasher were looted
And speeches made from the stage of the opera house
And the learned societies' papers were scattered over the
  forest and cast into the sea

Now the cells are as empty as holes in skulls
The prisoners who stayed on to live in the town lie in hillside
    graves under the pines
And there is an esplanade and a port open three months
    each year to cargoes
Brought on the sea on which it was said you could run to
    freedom and which made the rock tremble

The Traveller

A traveller fell into a ditch
A priest walked by
Help cried the traveller
Amen said the priest
In the end all lies in the grave
And walked on more slowly

When morning was afternoon
A general marched by
Help cried the traveller
Courtmartial roared the general
Talk in the trenches forbidden
And marched on more stiffly

When afternoon was evening
A merchant rode by
Help cried the traveller
Police cried the merchant
Cut-throats ! Wallet-snatchers !
And rode off as fast as his horse could carry him

When evening was night on that long day
A traveller came by
Help cried the traveller
In the morning he lifted him on his back
And carried him to the inn
But before then he had spent the night
With him in the ditch

Elegies

Elegies

The River

The spring comes from a stone mouth in the hills and makes
    its way
Somewhere it is a mirror – a man stares at his coloured
    shadow
Somewhere it is a hand carrying one can to the sea
Somewhere it breaks its banks and enters houses and drowns
    cars
The old mumble in consternation and the young fall silent in
    wonder
Till municipal workers hem it in and drive it back to the
    embankments
And for a few days the streets are awash with puddles as if
    giants had dried themselves there after bathing
In the ports great ships turn in their own shadows on
    hawsers as taut as shipping-line magnates' frowns and
    factory hooters yell
Ducks wade for weed and swoop on lunchtime crusts thrown
    by city clerks
On banks lovers find silence
Suicides stare into waters which are less than the tears they
    will never shed
The moon throws shadows under quays – they are like
    gloved fingers strangling the piers
The water washes staleness from dead mouths and stains
    from poisoners' hands
And joins the sea and carries the shoals and the trawlers and
    buries the shipwrecks
And the drowned sailors wander in it as it takes the victors
    home to parades
In the mountain it springs from the rock like a small hand

Gulls

Gulls follow the liner from New York to Southampton
They rested on the rails or hovered over it while it lay-to
Watched the old passengers and trunks and provisions
    landed
And new passengers and trunks and provisions taken aboard
When the engines were warmed-up they squalled and
    swooped over the decks
It left the quay – they followed it to the open sea
Always the same gulls
They'd chosen well – a luxury liner
The garbage and swill dropped overboard was rich in
    pickings
For four years the white birds followed the liner outward and
    homeward bound
When the brass bands and jazz combos and tearoom trios
    stopped you could hear them screeching
At night they slept on rails or rigging or the warm casings of
    worklights
Early in the fifth year it sank
A great pool of white water spread smoothly over the sea as
    if a sheet was laid for a giant picnic
And on it was spread a great feast from the stores and shops
    and abattoirs of the world
The gulls screamed and swooped and gorged on this
    abundance
Till they'd picked the sea clean
Then settled on driftwood and floating bodies still wrapped
    in evening suits and silk
Their clotted claws grasped diamond clasps as they preened
    their feathers
Then they must hurry back to land
It was a dangerous voyage
Storm winds blew many down into the waves
Some found new boats – a tramp and cargo steamers – some
    rested on wreckage
And in this and other ways
Many gulls came safely to land

Cities Should Sleep at Night

Cities should sleep at night
But so that the sick and wounded may be tended in hospitals
Bread be baked for the morning
Streets sprinkled and swept as clean as the faces of pupils
  who will hurry along them to school
Newspapers printed and stacked tied up in string on
  newsagents' doorsteps
The young dance and discuss till dawn
The lover wake the woman beside him
And the frowning stranger sit alone in the dark on the edge
  of a bed and ask why he came here –
That for this too there must be a place in the city –
And that it is good to sit over breakfast and read news from
  distant friends
For all these things the city must wake and work
The mailmen sort letters and parcels
Gangs of street-cleaners fill the sprinkler tankers with water
Sub-editors strike out government lies and PR exaggerations
And nurses watch
But otherwise let the city sleep
The miser shall not sit till the small hours to count his
  money and devour brokers' reports
Clerks hunch over forms or faulty computers
The keepers of small shops creep downstairs and reshuffle
  the tins on their shelves
Or furnace men with insect faces of goggles and scarves rake
  clinkers in showers of sparks
But let the contented and prosperous city sleep
While the stars stay in their ageless stories
And out in the fields the dog guards the flock from his
  brother the wolf

In The Atlantic With a Door

Far out in the atlantic
I swim with a wooden door
Sometimes I hold onto the edge with one hand
Sometimes I slide my arm under it and stick my hand up
    through the letterbox
Sometimes I lean on it with the top part of my body
Sometimes waves push me a few feet away from it
Sometimes I lie on it flat as if it were my bed – and then
    sometimes it overturns – the wood is sodden – and drops
    me in the atlantic
But when I surface I am never more than a few feet from it
Mostly the sea is bell-metal grey or the dark green of school
    corridors
But wind breaks grin-white crests
And the water that drains over the door is washing-up-liquid
    yellow
At night stars shine round the door like the eyes of a
    wolfpack waiting to enter the house
No food – I have nibbled the paint – I must be sparing with
    the wood
No rest – no part of my body or clothes is ever dry
This is not the story of a madman but of someone alone in
    the atlantic with a door
Or someone stooping to tie a shoelace in the street

Lovers

I wonder at the appalling stillness of lovers
They stand face to face on the busy street
Shoppers who would hoot at a wandering drunk
Glance at them furtively though they wouldnt know if they
    stared
They stand as if the world had stopped
A bullet could pass through them or a tank crush them in its
    embrace
A warrant could part them or police lead them to a van
They would welcome the handcuffs as if they were a lovers'
    knot
And see no danger till its too late
Love has no power inspite of the stories they tell of it
A few have died for love or built churches or hospitals
But to worship what gods and cure what diseases ?
Love has always been traded in worldly affairs
Now the lovers are still
One day they may run on this street and not notice it was
    the street where they'd stood
The executioner wiping his hands on the filthy towel has also
    stood in the street
Inspite of the stories they tell of it
Love has no power except over lovers

A Woman

I sat her in a comfortable chair
I shared my meal
I learned to listen carefully as she spoke of food and cooking
I fetched clothes for her from the high street
She showed great interest in the way buttons work and the
    size of pockets
She knows how to wash skin and is fastidious about the
    temperatures of water

She taught me to sweep floors as if I polished windows
She became quiet when I showed her my doorstep
She touched the unchipped corners and the dip in the centre
    where rain collects
She said it would not break underfoot
Since then she's taken to walking alone
When she comes back from faraway places she tells me about
    those who live there
How their houses are built – what they eat – and the manner
    in which they dress
She looks through palace windows but doesnt enter the gates
Why go into the cold when you can stay in the sun ?
But she listens carefully at the windows and when she
    returns she tells me what she has overheard
Then hurries away to tell her friends
She flows as easily as a river and is as strong as its banks
If she rests she's soon called from the street
She makes friends with things whose language I cant know
A loose bit of felt flaps – a car door slams – an empty can
    rolls on the sidewalk – and she runs off to her friends
She is not a prisoner to sit in darkness peering out through
    cracks in my head and overhear what she says and what's
    said to her
And grow old and crabbed and mad
But she rests in me when she's tired or stunned by what she's
    seen – though she's rarely stunned
When I wish to talk to her I must go out to the street
She runs to me calling the news and holding in out-stretched
    hands whatever she's found
Then she is intimate and because she's a stranger more of
    her is known
And more and more she looks at me from the faces of
    strangers I would never know
If she had not made them her friends

A Leaf

Seven months the green leaf held to the branch
In autumn it paled as it thought of death
Its stem shrivelled
And wind tore it and hurled it to the ground
We see emblems of time and decay
But who is to say the leaf would not have chosen this ?
Waited all summer long then tore loose from the trunk
Between thunder and split oak and stumps of branches felled
   by lightning
To dance in the streets like a child and soar over trees in
   mad winds
Over forests and rivers and roofs in its element of yellow and
   red
While the black clouds squeeze the sky till it pales
And the bare trees bend low over the grass and mourn their
   children who have gone to be free ?
Even now as it lies on the ground it curls to lift its head
And gaze at its own splendour

The Wooden Chest

This morning I woke
My left hand lay on the sheet over my chest
I was surprised to see how carefully it had been put there
    while I slept
The hand of a child and an old man
Age may be as deep in wonder as the child and a child
    calmly bear the cares of age
Stacked in a wooden chest there are many suits
Each more threadbare and mottled than the one before
The two silver buttons on each more worn
So that in the end the patterns are scratched and polished
    away
The oldest suit lies on the floor of the chest
Each morning we dress
And when our clothes are too small to cover us
Too worn to wear or too soiled to wash clean
We take the next suit from the chest
But no suit belongs to the same man
And each is older than the one that is laid aside
And as we put it on we wonder who first wore it
And put it in the wooden chest

War Shot

TV skeleton
Its shoulder half stuck from the mud as if it dragged the
    earth over it for a blanket and the bones of the free hand
    fingered the quality of the soil
By the wrist a line of pebbles

Then a robin hopped on the jaw
At once the mouth filled with fledgings' beaks shaking with
    the hunger of spears
In the stomach heavy dockleaves – cornflowers in the ribcage
I heard bees and a nearby stream
The white stones became a bracelet
Dry tears flickered on the screen

This Century

This century – a white flower opening in the dark
Hands reaching between passing trains
Pull the curtain – it falls at your feet – the rod hangs askew –
    light hits you like a boxer's smile
A good century for those who survive in it
The journeys were longer and the reports came back quicker
More seed was sown than in all the fields tilled before
    tractors
More tools were used than in all the homesteads and
    workshops before the time of technology
But when the owners and rulers saw how quickly we built
    with the new tools and how well we drove the new
    machines
They were afraid of our strength and saw that their time had
    passed
So they set us to earn our living wage by working with tools
    of destruction and driving the war machines
And learned to flatter the people

Contradiction

At dawn on four – at noon on two – at dusk on three – at
    night on none
And always at noon and dusk he may crawl on four or reach
    with a hand to the horizon as though it was a line thrown
    to him by his friends
How wisely he speaks ! – yet he studies rhetoric in the
    madhouse
Bakes mud and builds lawcourts – mows grass and thatches
    his settlement – raises cities and lives in their ruins
He teaches one child and pushes another under its mother's
    feet into the gas chamber
He carries his father on his back through the burning streets
    and loses him when he sets him down to rest by a quiet
    stream
The celibate assaults him yet even the celibate has the
    disciplines of the watchdog
He massacres innocents – they lie as cold as the snow – tears
    or time melt the snow – the murderers remain colder than
    their dead victims
He tends sheep and trains wolves for his sheepdogs
Naked and clawless he fells trees for stockades and on
    kitchen hearths smelts ore for arrowheads
With weapons stolen from graves grave-robbers send the
    living to their graves to be robbed
He scrawls his violence on walls and in libraries turns pages
    with the gestures of flocks rising from the stubble-fields of
    gleaners
In his dungeons death-rattles and chains sound like the
    abacus of the damned
He digs windows in basements and light shines on his towers
He chants in choirs and howls at his inhumanity
And when it is most dark he wipes a mirror with a hand it is
    too dark to see
And holds up an unlit torch so eager is he for the way

Clifftop

It had tilted on the clifftop
And emptied many graves into the sea
But it was still large enough to be a sheep field
Through centuries the village carried their dead to these
    heights
Their stones sank and lie underground like age-old waves
The romans were the first
After they had taken the land and made villeins of the people
Some buried here built the houses in which others still live
Otherwise all that is left of them is a few marks on deeds
At sea ships pass between ports divided by half the world
Gulls twist and call in the sky as if they looked down on a
    tragedy we cannot see
And though the rocks have stood through time in time they
    will fall
Or the sea go out and leave them as flesh leaves bones
Or they will fall and the sea go out
But now the white stones lie like faces on pillows
The peaceful remoteness of the pondering dead
I do not wish to think that's how they lived
But that they looked up when the gulls called

Here There Is No Evil

Between the hunting cackle of jays in the pine wood on the
    mountain
There is silence
The stag's head turns at each falling cone
A stream full of spies' eyes runs over the stones as
    indifferently as a machine
Birds sing in the open cages of oaks more massive than forts
The clearings are rife with poppies and bindweed
A fox slips from the shadow and brazenly shows its red in the
    hayfield
And there is no evil
The shepherd-hunter built his house of pine and with the
    sawn-off ends lit the first fire in the hearth
At evening he sits with his wife on the warm rock
Storms strike the mountain at night and by day grey wind
    blinds the women taking the children to school
And trees come out of the ground as if the world had been
    torn from their grasp
But still there is no evil
After the storm the fox slips from its den and the women
    stand on their porch steps and fasten their jackets as they
    set out to see the damage
And there is no evil
The beak was made for the apple not the apple for the beak
Men have to learn to build prisons before they deserve to be
    put in them
And many hands must carefully cut and stitch the beggar's
    rags
The mountain is strong – bound with forests and rocks
And shelters those who live on its side

In Praise of Rats

In the early morning before the traffic I sit on a bench
In the little garden at the north end of the Albert Bridge
Once leaves by the Thames were not black with grime
Shoots were not twisted like crippled fists and there were the
    flowers that flourish in wilderness
In one corner overfilled refuse bins and torn plastic sacks
And round them a litter of bottles and papers and human
    hair and a dance shoe
At the other end a stone wall retaining the earth
A rat falls from a crack between two stones
It dances and whisks its scaly tail
Twenty or thirty rats slip and drop through the cracks as if
    the wall dripped grey sweat
They feed on the grass that sprouts between the paving slabs
    close to the wall
Till one rat runs across to the garbage
Half-way there in the middle of no-man's land it stops
Then turns and shoots back through the dancing and
    whisking and feeding pack into the wall
Two seconds later the pavement is bare: the pack has gone
    as quickly as a tablecloth goes when one corner is pulled
    away
I smell of cordite
The wise rat knows danger
The pack was here before the garden and will survive the
    ruins

Tree

I thought that when time and rain and ice
Weakened the joints that held the limbs to my trunk
And most of them were always in winter
And would not bud again
And I grew so few leaves
That I could not hear them whisper
And heard more clearly the scurrying squealing animals
That burrowed in my roots
And old women said I was a good kindling-tree
And stooped to gather my fallen twigs
And birds did not nest in me because I was poor shelter
That then the bees would come
And live in my hollow trunk
Healing my raw wounds with their waxy combs
Frightening off the boys who would swing on my branches
For the excitement of falling when they tore from my trunk
And the farmer would not axe me
Because he could sell my honey
But the bees have not come
Instead the cold wind howls into my hollow
And curls up like a dog inside me and sleeps
And it could not be otherwise
Than that it should seek shelter
Where it can be found

Pier

At the far end of the pier one of the wooden pillars that rise
    from the sea to carry the frame of the deck
An iron band clasps it so tightly
That no matchstick admission-ticket dog-end or day permit
    to fish
Can be forced down between it and the wood polished by
    long neglect
The salt-corrupted metal is still solid under old daubs of
    iron-hard pitch
Near it a pillar bears the marks of an iron band
That one day sprang and fell with a cry into the sea
The seabirds scream and the fishermen count their catch
There is the unceasing sound of the waves
And the iron band
Clasps the pillar over the sea
And is as silent as the oracle that has spoken

Stony Ground

The old people knelt before stones
Set food on stone altars and asked for fair sea-weather and
    the return of sons from their voyages
Led cattle from auctioneers' hammers to priests' mallets and
    talked of trust among people
And prayed to the stones on which they sharpened their
    knives
That the fever would burn out and leave the green wood

We lay the wilderness waste and stack harvest-crates in the
    desert
Arm soldiers and trust peace to the generals
Think in the stone sedilla – teach from the stone lectern –
    cartwheel before the stone aedile
The stone dust on the sewer's hand stiffles the seed before it
    is scattered on stony ground
Yet it puts out shoots
That break stone and crack marble and split rock
And grows
And as we do not endure as long as rock we need not be
    broken
It is enough when seed is cast on stony ground that we tend
    it
Even the seed on stony ground
That we tend it

Starting a Play

Green claws push through the earth by the path under the
  trees
While you write aconites and snowdrops will flower
Birds seek holes and props for their nests
Days will lengthen as if each morning the white tablecloths
  were put out in a pavement café a little sooner
And you will make signs on these sheets
Typewriter-print corrected in ancient hieroglyphics of ink
This morning the mechanic nodded at me from the forecourt
During the month four cars will be towed from ditches
Repaneled and sprayed and driven away by their owners
Each evening the newspaper will come through the letterbox
  like a tongue poking from a fool's face
The receptionist in the local surgery will look out the records
  of two thousand patients
Many – new cards with sharp corners
Others – thick stapled wads with the grey fibre shredding
  inside the card where the corners are crumbled
Most of the patients will be ill for no longer than hours or
  days: a few will die
And the play will have been written
It is easy to write the truth
Except that we are asked to confess to others' crimes and tell
  their lies

Afterwards

At first the survivors lived in ruins or – as their ancestors
   who started our brief history – in caves
No medicine – the wounded and sick died
Wind and rain winnowed all toxins from the air
They leeched through the bottom of seas and ravines and
   burned in the furnaces at the earth's core
After a few generations no more infants were born defaced in
   the bomb's image
And people were wiser – after a flood no one believes in god
Neighbours and strangers dealt justly with one another and
   were given justice in return
The community had the means to manage but not to punish
Harvests were abundant as there were no rulers to sow blight
   and reap famine
And no wealth to buy discord
Men and women stood before each other in the beauty of
   their kind before bombs disfigured all flesh
The great insults were bomb-lover and button-jerker
There was peace in the cities and verdure covered the fertile
   stretches of land

Songs

Songs

Blackbird

Blackbird why do you sing
From your sharp beak notes as beautiful as the air
Blackbird why do you sing ?
    Other birds find my music fitting !

But we overhear your song
It worries us with unanswered questions
Of right and wrong
    O let me sing !

Venezuela

O go to Venezuela !
Where the grass is green
Where sirens call with such desire you swim to them in pity
O go to Venezuela !
Where silver bells hang on llamas' necks and shepherds read
    the books of sages
O go to Venezuela !
Where clouds hang like chandeliers in lakes and mountains
    stare at them in wonder
O go to Venezuela !
Where snow spreads picnic cloths for crowds on mountain
    tops
Where bandits wear their women's scarves and serenade
    them on guitars
Where tramps feet kick up pirates gold on shores and insects
    hum like devils' prayerwheels
And on mountain screes you read the poets' feet who hop
    with cranes and run with bulls
O go to Venezuela !
There in gothic libraries books whisper to each other the
    secrets of the roman index
And bats screech in the opera house
O go there !
In Venezuela comedians show you how Lear died and you
    will weep for pretty dancers spinning paper parasols on
    burning tightropes
In Venezuela the mechanics say they're building a bridge
    that will never end
O go !
Where the wind in high passes calls strangers by their
    nicknames and exile is home
O go – there or anywhere ! – but dont stay here

That With a Look or Nod

That with a look or nod
Or careless gesture of the hand
Or standing still or sitting in a chair
Or even as your shadow passes in the street
You take from the thin air
An iron rod and fierce flame
And brand me with your unknown name
And though from that day on we never meet
Yet I am turned to stone by your unseeing stare
And made a prisoner by the bait
That has no snare

Since Woman and Man

Two lovers walk in the street hand in hand
Slowly and silent as if asleep
As all lovers since woman and man
Then on the pavement they stop and kiss
In roaring traffic to find their bliss
As all lovers since woman and man

The Rose

I

I woke from a twilit sleep
Where a lost sea drove on an empty shore
And mute seabirds flew on the wind
And saw by my head
On the white untouched pillow
A red rose in a green dress
As if it had plucked itself
And come to lie in my bed

II

Red rose your petals and smiling lips
And your scented crown
The flesh of your mind and mind of your heart
Your stigma and stamen and whisp of down
Red rose that shines with the sheen of the hips
My hand gently folds your petals apart

III

The white finger touches your petals
And breaks one crystal drop of dew
And all the air is your odour
And later your odour and in my mind
The touch of your petals
Turns me at the door
To kneel again among
The petals that cover the floor

IV

Shall I give you the blood-red rose from the flowerbed
Or the white rose from the mystery of my head ?
I shall give you the red and white entwined
For man should give to woman his body and his mind

Song of the Bowl

With this bowl I feed you
With this bowl I drink you
With this bowl I bring you
With this bowl I take you
With this bowl I sleep you
With this bowl I wake you
With this bowl I tell you
With this bowl I speak you
With this bowl I sing you
With this bowl I flee you
With this bowl I chase you
With this bowl I laugh you
With this bowl I sorrow you
With this bowl I wait you
And when I am dead
And no more flee or wait or lust
With this bowl you can
Beg yourself a crust

Moon Song

Day in day out I turn two tides on earth
I draw the sheet to hide the dead
And lift the blanket from the baby's head
To show to friends
Year in year out my labour never ends
In summer heat and winter snow
In the fools' footsteps
And where the wisemen go
Each day I wash new foulness from the shore
But I am weary ! I can do no more !
I long to see that beauty on the earth
Men find in me
You children – make your world a place
That I may look on with a joyful face
So that my light will only show
Things I need not fear to know
And you will live in peace and love
And all the stars will long to fall
From this cold paradise above
Into the arms of earth below

Song of the Insane Tree

I am the tall tree of great girth
With giant branches spread
In the forest clearing
And when the boy that climbed me fell
I bent and my thick arms
Pinioned him to the earth
While I beat out his brains with a stick

And I would be a stately tree
But the wind bends my crown to the ground
And blows my arms round my head
I look up and see the sky in my ribs
And I would be better off dead

Sad Song

Suppose forever the earth stood still
No clouds moved
The wind was a handful of gravel scratching the sky
The trees turned in their own clockwork
The cherry was always in blossom and the pear in fruit
The animals stared at us with sullen dread
Because we had stolen their night
And birds hung over the lake
Where the moving waves were as hard as ice

Then through the still landscape I would go
By footprints that lay like chains in the snow
On the path to the dead volcano
By the sea changed to an idiot-child
Through cornfields where dry ears whispered old news
To the white-and-green churchyard where under the yews
Dead footballers sat on graves with no names

Better Said

No child without its mother's blood
And all born to wail
Not that the toil and pain
Are spent to no avail
But life is taken from the dead
Or it would be better said
The apple rises from the tree
And falls from the ground
But there's no resurrection for you and me
Birth comes from lust in bed
So do not wait – o do not wait !
Be cured before the wound

Song of the Old Sun

Traveller sun
Pale wanderer dressed in a cloud
Pale feet crossing the sand
White hair and white beard
Age bent on a stick
Tired traveller looking askance at the earth
That stirs under its shroud

Searching the empty house at night
For your daughter the moon
To swim in the seas of her plain
To heal the ache of your years
Old sun wandering barren mountains and seas
Lost youth going to age
For a moment you lean on your grave
A green shoot grows on your ankles and stick
Binding you to the earth

When in time you are old
And the earth is unhoused in the union of worlds
We will still hold it in our hands
As we hold an infant to set it to crawl
Pale sun you will shine as if time returned
Death will be feared no more
And men and women will play
As children play on the shore

In art and skill we seek to imitate the sea
To calm ourselves with rage as the sea rages to be calm
We search for the quiet coast where the light shines
On waves and rocks and sand
Where we will go without stumbling
As if we walked on the sea not the land

Morning Song

It is said that spring will come
And tomorrow the sun will rise
But on what will the light fall ?
And who will open their eyes ?

Each day you must rise when you wake
And feed the sea at your door
And teach the trees in the wood to speak
Or the sun wont rise any more

So sit down with the cup and plate
And eat the breakfast bread
And send the children to play
And sweep the house of clay
And your hands give light to the day

Burying Song

He was rocked in the cradle
And in his father's and mother's arms
When love burned brightly his body rocked
As waves run from the river boulder
Rock him on your shoulders now he is dead
Rock him as a boat rocks in the sheltered mooring
The leaves on the wreathes shake from your tread
And let even your tiredness rock him a little
As you lay him in his earthly bed

Three Cruel Songs

1. Song of the Knife

I have killed presidents on marble steps
And desperate women in dark alleys
Flayed saints and tortured innocents
Been carried aloft in processions
And frantically buried in mud
Fathers have struck me into sons
And sons into fathers
I have silenced those who laugh
And those who weep
Cut the throats of children and sheep
Been wiped on statesmen's handkerchiefs
And executioners' towels
I know the beat of the human heart
And the grip of the human bowels
The blood I have shed would drown the sea
My dead would bury the land
All places of stench and foulness are known to me
But where do I most shudder to be ?
In the human hand

2. Song of the Whip

He whipped me from my mother's side
He whipped me at the plough by day
He whipped me to the stall at night
He whipped me while I ate my hay
He whipped me when I bore the yoke
He whipped me when my hide was raw
He whipped me till the whiplash broke
And then he beat me with a cane
He whipped me when the prices fell
He whipped me when he reeled with drink
He whipped me till the blood ran down
And I was lame and old and weak
And there was no more pain
At last he whipped me into town
And tied me to the butcher's door
I smelt the sweat and heard the groans
And stood in blood that washed the floor
I wept and trembled ! I was sold
The man went off and drank my price
The butcher slew me with his knife
Then hacked the hide from off my bones
And I was stretched and dried and cut
And tied into a knout
And now Im used for whipping men
I lash them while they beg and shout
I flog them screaming Faster ! Faster !
Now you're the beast and Im the master !

3. Song of Lucian the Lawyer's Clerk

I sit behind my master's desk
And humbly smile at the rich and great
At the weak who fawn on the strong
And the poor who wait at the gate
One makes a will that disowns an heir
Another buys love with a Deed of Hate
A crook swears an oath to betray a friend
A servant hangs for his master's crime
And statesmen barter the state
   I merely smile and bide my time
   For my time will come in the end

I sit behind my master's desk
Many pass but none of them see
That as I smile I open my book
And write in my inventory
And by each name I record each crime
Each oath – each lie – each treason
Each drop of blood – each tear that's shed
Who's sold in the street – who's bought in bed
I write it down for this reason –
One beautiful morning I shall die
And go to the angel who sits in the sky
And writes all you do and all you say
In the book to be opened on judgement day
And I shall tell him all that he missed
And make him scribble till his pages
Are blacker than sin with your crimes and outrages !
   All that I saw from my desk I shall tell
   So that when I die you go to hell

Angry Song

You break your brother's bones when you are told
You think you walk in freedom when you're sold
To the red-handed butcher
Yes ! you run to fetch his tackle and hook
And write your name in his invoice book
And sharpen the blade and hand him the knife
And stand in the sluice and give him your life
You live and die in this slavery !
And your death-rattle cry is Liberty !

Song of Success

Why am I so cold ?
The wind is as harsh as giants blowing on their nails
The roots are barbed-wire frozen in the ground
The gull hops and flutters – its frozen wings cant fly
The sun is a livid frost-bite in the sky
Why am I so cold ?
Im frightened by the idea that comes in my head
That keeps me awake in the middle of the night
Drench yourself in petrol then set yourself alight
I know I would not be so cold if only I were dead

Trainer's Song

The trainer turned the bird's feathers to lead
Then asked it what it had learned
He pointed his gun at it and said
Fly away bird or you'll be dead !
The bird tried to fly
It fluttered and fell
The trainer put a bullet in its head

The trainer turned the fox's legs to steel
Then asked it to show what it could do
He blew his horn – the hounds came to heel
Run away fox ! Give yourself a start !
The fox tried to run
It staggered and fell
The hounds yelled as they pulled the fox apart

The trainer taught the people to obey
Then asked them what they had learned
We know how to kill and how to pray
We'll be safe when the enemy attacks
We'll bolt underground or run away
And our rockets are waiting in the racks

The Destitute Woman

They turn the river to cement and ask why the water doesnt
    flow
They chain the prisoners to the walls and tell them they're
    free to go
They turn the leaves on the trees to lead and wonder why
    they fall to the ground
Dont ask questions – it's too late now – just lie still and dont
    make a sound

The grass didnt choose to grow in the dirt
Or shells to lie on the shore
The slaves cry out when the shackles hurt
When they're dead they wont hurt anymore

So grab from the shelves you who're hungry and cold
And raise your fists when you're mad
Dont be good and do what you're told
Its time for the good to be bad

I passed a woman alone on the street
Her face was a shivering stone
The tower blocks were tall – she had rags on her feet
I heard the traffic groan
There were planes in the sky – and on that street there
    hurried this creature of bone
She passed offices and shops and steel-barred banks
Her head was bowed and she muttered one word: thanks
And went on her way alone

Fallen Bells

The bells rang out in the tower
Till the day the tower fell
Then the bells were buried in rubble and dust
Their mouths were choked with bricks and rust
People climbed over the ruins
The sick and wounded and lame
Over the bells in the ground
And no one remembered the terrible sound
When the bells peeled high in the air
To warn them that the fire was coming
That their city would be turned into hell

People walked over the rubble
Over the bells in the ground
They could not ring a requiem
Though the city was a burial mound
And no one remembered the joyful sound
Before the city fell
When the bells rang high in the air
Filling the city with their singing
In the days when all was well

Mother's Song

I had a child – they said another brat
Another mouth to feed – and what's the use of that ?
I worked all day – all night you'd cry and choke
Although I nursed you till the morning broke
What use were you to me – a bundle of old rags ?
Yet on those rags there was a button – bright !
The thread that fastened it would never break – or fray !
Although the world hung from it on a chain
But what's the use of that – a diamond on old rags ?
You ask me why – what can I say ?
I know that mountains crumble in the wind and rain
And so I gave my child away

They said your kid – we'll feed and dress it well
Let us take care of it – dont keep it in this hell
We'll keep it clean – and teach it wrong from right
We'll train it to behave and make it sleep at night
What use were you to me – a bundle of old rags ?
Yet on those rags there was a button – bright !
The thread that fastened it would never break – or fray !
Not if the world hung from it on a chain
But what's the use of that – a diamond on old rags ?
You ask me why – what can I say ?
I know that mountains crumble in the wind and rain
And so I gave my child away

You dont give statues bread
Or water to the dead
Yet you give soldiers guns
And send them out to play
And sometimes mothers
Give their child away

Children Sit Bowed At Your School Desks

Children sit bowed at your school desks
The prisoner's safe in his cell
The rich man rides to his factory
The street traders haggle and sell
The tanks stand guard at the frontier
The sentries keep watch in the night
Children bow low at your school desks
And learn to read and write

Children add sums on your fingers
The judge is washing his hands
The soldiers are taught to pull triggers
The officers to bellow commands
Are they trenches or graves they're digging ?
And why have they cordoned the square ?
Children bow low and write at your desks
When you look up the streets will be bare

Children stand to salute the flag
That flaps on the hangman's rope
Dont ask what your fathers are making
In the factory outside the town
There has to be food for the table
And a roof to cover your head
And doctors to call when the roof's blown down
And flowers for when you are dead

Children bend low and study
The world will go on its way
The rockets are aimed in their silos
So its safe to go out and play
And when the rockets are fired
And your city burns day and night
You'll be bent very low at the school desks
Where you learned to read and write

Children sit bowed and study
Let the world go on its way
Dont ask what your fathers are making
Its safe to go out and play
The wind whistles over the barbed wire
Your enemies live far away
They dont walk beside you as you go home
And watch over you all the day

My Child Its Not Only You Who Cries

My child I sit beside you at table
And carefully put the food on your plate
I smile as you play with your friends in the street
And stand by your bed and watch you sleep
I look at my empty hands and wonder
I hear the rumbling in the skies
Are the old stories of thunderbolts true ?
Do gods punish men for their violence and lies ?
My child its not only you who cries

I'd make the whole wide world your table
And give you the harvests of orchards and fields
I'd let you climb to the highest tree top
The mountains would watch you while you sleep
I look at my empty hands and wonder
I hear the rumbling in the skies
Are the old stories of thunderbolts true ?

Do gods punish men for their cruelty and lies ?
My child its not only you who cries

Solomon

Two neighbours bore a son
Within a few days of each other
One was in debt and in her misery
Got drunk and slept across her child
It died like rain falling into the sea
She woke and crept into her neighbour's house
And stole the baby from its sleeping mother

The case was sent to court
The wise judge called – My sword !
And when it had been brought
He lifted it and said
I'll cut the child in two from toe to head
Each mother shall have half when it is dead
But one said Yes the other No
Imprison me but let the baby go
And I shall see it playing in the street

Then the judge gave the child
Back to its true mother
One wept the other smiled
But the judge said – Good people it is wrong
That the rich rob the poor
And the weak bear the strong !
He struck off all the weeping woman owed
And had these words carved on the judgement door

The mother gave justice in this court
Rather than be cruel to her son
She would have let the law do wrong
She showed that love and justice may be one
Let us learn justice from those whose feet
Write it each day in dirt on the common street

Dont Die for Them

Dont die for them !
A hundred million dead !
They couldnt sleep in bed
With that number in their head
If they tried to make a speech
They'd be struck dumb or cry
Till their howling filled the sky
If they knew the pain it cost
A hundred million dead to die
Dont die for them !
They don't know what they're doing !

They get on with their life
Swilling grub and swigging wine
With no doubts in their head
They're pleased with their new way of killing
One moment you'll be there
Standing in the line
Then you'll vanish into air
You wont feel it more than swine
Killed in the butcher's shed
If you linger on in pain
They'll put a bullet in your brain
You can thank them when you're dead
And they're stuffing grub and swilling

Dont die for them !
Take the bread from the rich
In this century the poor should eat
Take the weapons from the strong
In this world they belong to the weak
Take the prisoners from their cell
Let the suffering out of hell
Dont die for them !
Brother ! Sister ! Comrade ! Friend !
Dont die for them
And the long long war will end !

Peace Song

Peace is a city built at the place
Where the beast turns back from the slaughter
And tramples the priests who wait
With knives and blood on their face
And the warrior kings turn pale
At the omens dealt to their race
     It runs from the stones where its brothers lie dead
     And its sisters' entrails are read
     And a green grove will grow on the path where it fled
     From the olive branches that fall from its head

Song of the World

The kings and crowns shall come to dust
The swords and spears be blunt with rust
Red as the blood of foe and friend
The mountains sink into the seas
The tyrant stumble to his knees
All things shall find their end
And on the ground or under it
Lie like the ashes of the pit
All things shall fall
And yet it matters more than breath or life
That we live justly with each other
And carve on rocks the laws of humankind
For those who follow us to find

Song of Time

Time ! – you clothed your nakedness
With my scrap of life
Stained with the sweat of forefathers
And the tears of strife
And when the first rough wind is blown
I will not fall away
To let you snatch some other child
To cover your bones
I'll stay

I was torn from the bough before I was born
I will not be scattered now
That you need a death for your mirth
Time ! – you bore me so you could live
But I shall not leave the earth
Till joy and peace shall make my death
For those who follow me
Birth

Satires

Satires

I walked in the field
Back – cried the skeletons – our trenches !
I walked on the water
Abuse from captains of passing ships – trespassers
   prosecuted !
I flew
Heckled by a flock of crows – cant build a nest !

God's in his heaven the devil's in hell
Why dont things in this world go well ?
If god was to fall and the devil to rise
If children stopped singing and the damned didnt moan
If the sun didnt set and the moon didnt wane
Things might go well with the world again

Sighing with care I saw a dog
Its tail swinging low
Enter a wood with a bone in its mouth
Happiness is still possible

The hawk is patient in the air
The spider is patient in the web
The daffodil nods its head
And I count your days
The poppy said

A man ran to the churchyard each saturday morning and
   yelled
Im alive !
One night he came home late and set fire to himself
To find his key

Zen says rope round man's neck stops him falling –
   sometimes better to fall
Zen says those who tie rope round neck and kick stool but
   carry knife to cut rope in case no one come – beware jolt of
   rope knock knife from hand

Man didnt fall he was pushed
Evil has the power we give it
Madness ? – the music of sanity syncopated by the tapping of
   prisoners on walls

Zen says match decided between rounds while boxers sit in
   corners and exchange glances
No. 2 skater becomes ice she skates on – No. 1 waits till ice
   melted
We sing before we know tunes worth singing
Pencil too close to see drawing
Eyes that gaze on rope become nets
Roadmaker cant lose way – road follows him
If roadmaker lose way – stand still – road catch him up
Few have such patience

If the messenger smiles when you open the door
It is too soon to be glad
He may only smile to calm you before
He tells you the news is bad

The swan is white the blackbird is black
When Jack loves Jill Jill may not love Jack

Its the workers' sunday morning
We're screwing in time to the bells
Calling the pious to press cold knees
On hassocks in cold churches
While the priest pokes his fingers in the air
To find a blessing

Absurd and flagrant the timid hare
Exposes itself in the mating dance

When man first woman saw his heart began to sing
And neither knew the iron chain that hangs from the golden
    ring

A disciple isnt master of himself
What master wants such a disciple ?
Let all teach and learn
And this should be taught first
Deceit travels as the disciple of truth

Mostly it happens
Since people are in the wrong places
That the waiter knows more about food than the diner
But it is the diner who complains of the cook
Not the waiter who complains of the diner's manners

In the haunches of the sphinx it is written
The art of the past is useful – use it
But dangerous if you mistake it for
The art of the present

It is a condition of despair
When the writer is forced to live in his imagination
Homer Virgil Dante Cervantes didnt

Zen says to see sitter artist must see how sitter will see
      portrait
Artist's eyes empty begging bowl till passers-by drop coin

The owl the wolf and the nightingale
I am complete
The owl for wisdom and watching
The wolf for swiftness and nurturing young
The nightingale

They chant in the desert and wait
For the echo from the mirage

The opera company's coach has crashed on the motorway
Lies on its side – wailing of well-trained voices
Explodes – fanfare of instruments
Minister of arts issues a statement
      How well we nurture the arts !

In the fire the comic and tragic masks buckle and twist
Later they have exchanged expressions

Operas of death
Funerals of space
Ashes of the phoenix
Now a shortage of boxes

In winter naked trees – chattering branches – beggars' teeth
In summer green boughs – blossom – girls dressing for
      weddings
As with the rich so with the poor
He that hath takes from him that hath not
So he shall have more

He was a cunning man and did not steal
He walked in orchards on windy days

When the poor steal from the rich
Its like trying to get rings off jugglers' fingers

Which profession calls for more skill
Stealing or poverty ?

Zen says only poor know why dead dont eat coin in mouth
(Need it for protection money in hell or taxes in heaven)

What a world !
They make a ruin and shore it up with our bodies
They wipe up their mess with our uniforms
They tell us to walk on water and then prop up the sky with
    our hands
Im off to the supermarket – if the checkout girl cheats me
    again I'll know its all up with us !

A youth face-down in the gutter after the match
Judge – have you no conscience ?
Accused – how d'you spell it ?

Runway – dew on the shell case
A green tendril grows over the yellow flash
A member of ground crew ties on his flying scarf and goes
    into town
A girl wipes the counter top – the urn hisses
Nations are lost

In europe africa asia
In all the missionary lands
In all the churches
Not one reliquary – not one – in which is worshipped
A piece of the scourge that drove from the temple
The hordes of moneymen

Moral principles might have saved the ship
While the captain jerrymandered compromises
With pirates rocks squalls and all other dangerous obstacles
In hailing distance

When the cracks in their world were so wide
That they walked on their floors
They thought they were new lands
Their armies had conquered or their companies bought

The day has wreathed its venom on our brows
Emptiness obstructs us in the doorway
By the wayside the world bends in a blade of grass
Let us go where we dont have to grimace in the monkey's
    court
Where the sky hangs like a lantern over the storm

The blade of grass shivers
It is not cold
It is not famished
It has not heard the marching feet
Or the dictator's screams
The blade of grass shivers

By the road
Fur flesh and viscera weathered away
Bones in the shape of a weasel
A necklace of death in the grass

They use the eyes of a child for a gutter
And when it has grown used to the nails they knock in its
    coffin
They pull them out
And knock them into its cross

There is a chasm so deep
It is dangerous even to walk
Towards it

The emperor strutting in new clothes
Is preceded by a flagpole on which flutters
A strip of the same material

The generalissimo had one doubt of god his maker
That from eden there came no line of stately trees
On which grew axes

In the distance a ruined village
Fallen walls like clothes thrown down in fields
The giants are swimming between attacks

Water sea stone
The shouts of murderers carrying dead into prison cages on
    the shore
The panic of hostages on the sunlit square

The suddenness of rage
The silence of stones
The greeks are children
They say tomorrow

After a long war minds are soured
Children talk like politicians
Politicians laugh like children
Hate settles like dust

The giants have eaten
Their empty plates are menacing

Dante saw in the soot of human bones
A human footprint and wept

Spinoza I remember
Who ground lenses
In the anvil a heart that cannot break

The tyrant hopes that imprisoned long enough you forget the
    shape of the sun
The square cell reminds you

The white pigeons are dark in the clear sky
A few pale flecks at the collar and breast
In the storm they are white

In the iron land only the gods laugh
But whoever laughs is god

The government must purchase ten thousand bars
Break two – you are free to attack the prison

By this stream women shivered and men wept
I stoop to wash my face in the discarded helmet
Using the inside of the mask
And my fear goes

You say the water we give you to drink is clouded
We had to wash the cup
Drink friend – you are thirsty

Discourses

Discourses

In Praise of the Simple and Clear

In the silence between thunder the dry grass whispers
In the storm you may hear rivulets run by the feet of ants
After great wars a woman sits on a chair in front of her door
    to watch the evening sun
And a child with its chin on its knees writes with a stone in
    the road

In the knot the rope is bound to itself
One force holds another so that the rope pulls with itself and
    against itself
To make a new force that holds the boat fast to the swift
    mooring
And the forces can be plainly seen in the knot

The first people understood many things – in caves ideas
    were used with precision
In prisons there are ideas torturers cannot reach
And in the heads of the condemned taken to be shot there is
    knowledge
That later brings down the official who signed the warrants
    for execution

I love all that is clear
Great men would have destroyed the world and philosophers
    driven us mad
If people had not stood on the streets with their child on
    their arm and its arm round their neck and told each other
    about their lives

And stopped in shop doorways on their way home from work
   to pass judgement

It is true that workers have killed each other so that their
   masters might prosper
And as their child lay sick in rags marched in uniform
   through streets of bunting
While their master's child – propped in its parent's arms
   with an arm round its mother's neck – waved a flag at
   them from a window
As the child breaks toys so the master breaks people and
   their accord with each other

When the puppet dances look for the strings so that your
   eyes are led to the puppeteer
Crowds have marched to war or church or work dangled on
   strings held in skeletons' hands
We should accustom ourselves to see who dangles on strings
   held in skeletons' hands

For always there are these simple things
Reason and careful judgement and listening before and after
   speaking
Cherish all that is simple and clear
Things obscure or hidden or dark are not treasures of
   untellable wisdom
But violence against people to persuade them they cannot
   learn to be human
And take their lives from them

Praise all that is simple and clear
Things as broad as the sea and deeper than lines that fathom
   oceans
When water is taken from the deep and cupped in the hands
It is clear
And this truth changes the world and shows us how to live

Democracy

In the great war soldiers bleated as they marched to the front
What is the state of soldiers who fight for freedom and bleat ?
They are not as free as prisoners and slaves
Prisoners see chains and bars – slaves see whips and hear
    curses
The soldiers knew their officers were their enemies
But if they had fled from the trenches their officers would
    have shot them in the back
Slaves strike the overseer while his back is turned and leave
    him stretched in the field
Prisoners dig their cell floor while the guards sleep
To be free the soldiers would have to fight their officers face
    to face
Instead they marched – and bleated to show they knew they
    were slaves sent to die for their enemies' freedom
Other soldiers marched to the front and whistled – and their
    officers marched at their side to die with them at the front
What is the state of the soldiers who marched and whistled ?
Worse than the state of prisoners: they did not see their cells
Worse than the state of slaves: they did not hear the whips
Worse than the state of soldiers who marched and bleated:
    they did not know their enemy
Worse than the state of the officers who marched to die by
    their side at the front: the officers died for their fathers and
    children who were the owners of slaves and the keepers of
    prisons
The whistling soldiers died for their enemies and imprisoned
    their fathers and drove their children to slavery
Prisoners who do not know they are in prison lie in the
    strongest cell
Slaves who do not know they are slaves bear the heaviest
    chains

Being Human

Standing opponents against a wall is a primitive way to rule
And good factories produce more than slave camps
The old paradox that a man might be free in prison is not
    true
But a man who is not in prison might not be free: many
    democracies are tyrants
Democracy is not freedom to walk the streets or work or
    inherit wealth
Or even freedom to speak if the slave lies for his owner
Democracy is knowledge – it protects truth and cannot
    defend the right to lie
Guard your mind against lies as you keep foul water from
    your mouth
Cows are not cattle because they have hoofs and hides – they
    are cattle because butchers have knives
We are not human because we have hands and minds – we
    are human when our mind knows what our hands do
When workers sell their hands to their owner he fills their
    mind with his teaching – then they go to work quietly and
    are grateful when from what they produce they are
    allowed to keep the means to live and then there is no
    democracy
How strong are the owners ?
The owners say their culture is the light of humanity – as
    natural as the day – yet it keeps you in darkness
They say they are armed to defend you yet you bear their
    arms so that they are free to enslave you
Democrats – the power you give your owners is greater than
    the power of all the tyrants who filled the prisons and all
    the despots who traded in slaves before you were born !
Slaves break the chains and prisoners throw down the walls
But for democrats imprisoned in slavery it is hard to be free
They forge the chains and build the walls that imprison them
Yet we must struggle to be free: how else shall we be
    human ?

Understanding the River

When the banks are neglected the river floods
Even on calm days those who live on the banks tremble
But those who work on the river must live on the banks

Reeds shake in the shallows and fish have fins
Such things are the law of the river
And those who live on the banks and catch fish must also
    obey the law of the river
No one is born corrupt yet on still nights curses and blows
    are heard in the fishermen's village and lanterns swing in
    the twisting lanes as if they shook in a hurricane
And each day in the market fishermen catch fishermen
These things happen because the law of the river shapes the
    fishermen's lives
As surely as water turns the wheel in the mill-race

There is an old story of oppressed people who took a river
    from those who neglected its banks
And mastered it so they could choose between good and evil
    and learn to be human
And you who live in great cities – stand like the fishermen on
    the bridge and look down in the river white with the rage
    of the flood
And there is your image struggling and clawing in the angry
    water !
You work in great towers and factories yet you live on
    crumbling quays and each day fall from the bridge and are
    swept away in the flood !
Look at your city where friend betrays friend and the
    violence of day is worse than the violence of night !
Your cities are great – your towers are tall – your workshops
    are busy – but the law of the little fishermen's river is also
    the law of great cities and your towers will be washed
    away by a trickling stream !

You are no freer than fishermen who crouch and shiver in
   river mud !
Than corpses that float on the water !
Till like the fishermen you take the river from those who
   neglect it
And as you learn to control it it will teach you to be human

The Wheel

The wheel takes the king's chariot swiftly to battle
Past the foot-sloggers and over the dead
Slowly the haycart rumbles into the barn
Its wheels rattle like execution drums and kings' heads fall at
the village pump
The frigate takes the cannon to the enemy fleet and cargo-
decks carry the wounded
The factory owner sledges down his heap of gold and the
worker walks home in the dross of the day
And in the workshop the ponderous steam-hammer nods
over its world of gears
A way of life changes – those who live it change – the old is
made new
In the night a man stumbles and clutches at the dark for
support
In the morning he holds a pole in his hand and over his head
a banner opens
In the crowded suburbs each house becomes a garrison
Each doorway a checkpoint
Each roof a lookout
Each purchase of food provisions an army
Each gesture of anger or resolution beckons change to come
faster
Soon the enemy will retreat to their fastness in the hills
They do not find safety
As they climb the hairpin bends they take their enemy with
them: themselves
Soon speakers stand at street corners and newspapers
printed on second-hand presses – the ink very black and
the paper very white – are handed out to the listeners
And men and women drag chests to the centre of rooms and
bend over the open lids and hand guns to those who stood
unarmed before soldiers
And the revolution will have a face at every window
Because the world turns in the orbit of wheels

The Pneumatic Drill

With a borrowed spade a man digs his grave in his owner's
    land
Loyally he vows that when he falls ill he will walk to the
    grave
To spare others the burden of carrying him
In time he walks to the grave and climbs in
The priest calls him unsung little saint of the people
His wife and son shed tears on the soil
The owner puts the spade in the son's hands

The owner sends the son to war
The son digs mass-grave trenches that spare the owner the
    cost of quartering armies
Is the son angry before he dies ?
He feels the rain that falls on him

The owner puts a pneumatic drill in the grandson's hands
When the grandson sees the rain fall on his forefathers'
    trenches and graves
What does he do ?

Two people: A a worker and B an owner
What happens to A cannot happen to B
What happens in A cannot happen in B
A and B know the world differently
The world gives them different minds
A and B are in different worlds
There is a logic even to fantasy: A can imagine rationally but
    what B imagines must be irrational
Any A who tries to be B is an owner who owns nothing: he
    disowns his world and his mind

In the past both the owner and mason could imagine that
  stone came from the gothic hand of god
But cement is A-made
Cement is not poured in libations to the glory of god
Cement honours cement works and cement workers
B speaks a dead language
The pneumatic drill is an oracle that tells A to make a new
  world
In A's hand the pneumatic drill abolishes the owner
A abolishes B

The Foyer of the Royal Court Theatre

Drama is not an event in life such as buying a coat
It is an event about life – as the actor acts buying a coat the
  act asks: who are you who watch ?
As you judge the play you judge yourself – the appetite
  knows its teeth
In history two things meet – the will of the living and the will
  of the dead
Reason allows us to be human even in our struggle with the
  will of the dead
It is always a question of ideas – one hates the crime another
  honours and one dies for the cause another betrays
The forces that bring the world into being are also the forces
  of history
Beasts and grass stand in the same field and suffer the same
  change
But we create change – we enslave ourselves in the morning
  and free ourselves at noon and may enslave ourselves in
  the evening
The actor shows a character – this character – inner and
  outer – is political – it cannot be otherwise
And the spectator is formed in the same way and it cannot
  be otherwise – the inner and outer – political
The past is always public – when the agonies and the joys
  are gone the decisions remain

So it is with the present – when we act privately we act in
   history
And politics is the history of the present
It is the way in which we create our humanity or bear the
   consequences of our inhumanity
When our ideas are formed in reason we may be happy – our
   passions will flourish and we will walk without despair on
   the slope of grey shifting shingle above the shore of the
   tragic dead
Pause when the play is over – judge later – not by what you
   wish but by what it is wise to wish – not the appetite or
   even the hunger but the teeth
History is partisan
The unbiased are fanatical – they have the faith of madmen
The dramatist cannot be impartial – nor may you
You must tell the truth as you know it – in this way you
   judge yourself
And the truth is forced from you even by fiction

John Clare Eats Bread – or That is How You Wished it to Be

They love each other
Can they feed each other ?
Life is hard and there's little work but for a time the room is
   dry and they eat
So they love
But the landlord peers through the cracked window and
   tonight he puts down his list of sackings
Soon there's no work and no bread and a leaking roof
Voices rise in recrimination
Neighbour preys on neighbour
And the street is sullen with anger

First you see John Clare eat with his wife
Later he sells her for bread and cheese
You are surprised to see the good neighbour who cherished
  his family sell his wife so that he can eat ?
But that is how you wished it to be !
Doesnt a man have to sell his family and neighbours to eat
  and waste his humanity for the roof over his head ?
Worse – when your neighbour's plate is emptier than yours
  havent you stolen your bread from him and his children ?
There is no other way in the world it could have got on your
  plate
But no one shouts thief
You eat because your master pays you and because you eat
  you love
In this way your master lays down the whole of your life
A master is not made good because you take his money or a
  law made just because you obey it
How can you judge what is just or good – or sane ?
If you see the world through your master's eyes you are like
  a man who thinks he is someone else
As confused as a clerk who thinks he's napoleon
How can such people live peacefully side by side in the
  streets of a madhouse ?
You say your city is violent ?
But that is how you wish it be be !
You are a thief who shouts thief
So do not complain when one day you huddle in a corner of
  your dry room with your arms round the ones you love
  and stones break your windows as if they etched in the
  glass the face of rage !
That is how you wished it to be

And that is why I show you how John Clare eats bread

The Manner in Which Justice is Spoken

Each sessions the judge came in his gallows clothes
A trumpeter before and town dignitaries behind
To eat and drink at a feast for which the town paid
Till the town abolished the feast
But the judge decreed it should be held
He paid for the meat and wine
The trumpeter went before
And the dignitaries sat at his table
They drank to the judge not to justice
There could be no justice in the court of a judge
Who walked in pride in his gallows clothes
And spoke a dead language
It would be better if an old man or old woman
Walked through the streets to court
Leaning on a stick and carrying
A few books in a rucksack
And the people followed
And all sat in judgement
And the words of justice were spoken simply
Where justice wears gallows clothes
Crow-black and bone-white
We should take its rags and books
And burn them on the marble steps of the court
And let all who go there for justice
Tread the soot into the halls and courtrooms
To remind those who judge
Of the price of injustice
Justice has often lain in prison
The bolts are massive
The stone blocks are strapped with iron
Her cell is reached through a tunnel cut in the rock
Daylight does not pass through the keyholes
And yet with an uproar of people
Justice is freed
Her angry protectors march through the streets
Breaking windows and looting and burning
And sometimes people are trampled to death in the gutters

But others are so long enslaved
They cant raise their voices or even their eyes
To their master
But creep before him as if they were blind
And bow lower than they bowed in labour
And when he is brought before them on the threshing floor
They whisper so that justice is hardly heard
'My master – the hut we rent –
Wet – my wife – fever – died
My son asked for justice
Soldiers shot him'
But when they have learned to shout the charges
They are shouting the name of
Justice !
And they may take down the flails
From their nails on the walls
And winnow the blood of his limbs onto the threshing floor
Till he is as spent as the mildewed seed in his storehouse
And because we have read the law books
And talked with philosophers
Shall we say this is not justice ?
It is also justice
But hurry to build a place
Where justice is stern and quiet
For when all live for each other
Wisdom is stern and merciful
And justice is simple
Not spoken in anger
But in the quiet voice of truth
Using the language in which no lie can be spoken
Let the factory workers leave their benches
Wearing work-shirts but clean and the collar open
Let the gardeners scrape and oil their tools
And go through the garden gate
Let the clerks come from their offices
And justice will not frown if a mother
Is folding her apron as she enters the courtroom
Then what need is there for the old man and old woman
The sandals and rucksack and stick ?
Let all hurry to speak justice

Justice is written in simple words
If the books of justice are long
And the language picked over in footnotes
As a cat searches for fishbones in a dustbin
If old words are used in argument
When their common meaning is lost
And oaths are sworn to dead gods
Then these things are used like a pickpockets' coat
To conceal crime not reveal it
They cover anger with smiles
And violence with polite gestures
And the accused stands in a thieves' den
Waiting for justice
When the judge speaks a dead language
And dresses in actors' clothes
And justice is locked in the courtroom
There is no justice
Then hurry to make the books simple
Justice must speak in all human dealings
Be plainly seen and plainly spoken
The voices raised at the workbench must speak justice
The miner in his shaft must shout for justice
The mechanic will not need to dress in gallows clothes
Before he can speak justice
Or the salespeople sell in one language
And speak another in courtrooms
When all speak justice the judge will be just
For justice is a language in which no lie can be spoken
Justice is subtle but not twisted
Profound but not hidden in books
Such things are the masks of injustice
Justice is made as the sculptor works stone
With a hammer and chisel chipping at pieces
As if they were links in a chain
Till justice steps from the block
With her hand and towel and bowl all in one carving
And the water in the bowl as clear as air
Do not be afraid of this world: it is also the place of justice
Justice is simple and waits in the stone
But it must be chiselled free

Or hammered from chains
And then justice will be spoken
In the homes and factories and streets where it is learned
And then at last it will be spoken in courts of justice
It is one language
And when the accused is called he will come to court without
    escort
He will not be threatened by bailiffs but he will pay his fine
Or if he is sent from home he will bid goodbye to the
    neighbours
Who will welcome him when he returns
For justice will be given to him by his friends and spoken in
    his own language
For there is always justice
Justice ! Justice !
The language in which no lie can be spoken

The Lie Concerning Self

The last secret is the lie concerning self
Here language lags and poetry may create understanding

That we are the one and the others the many
That the crowd is a monster
Half-eaten people hang from its maw
Their legs and feet writhe and kick at the ground
Slither and scrape – and this is how the monster moves
    forward
The feet of those it devours struggling to get free push and
    drag the stomach that devours them
So that it always moves forward – always grasping more
    victims
Always voiding the cannibal shit in its bowels and is never
    still and never dies
That is the lie concerning the many

Perhaps when a man drowns in the ocean its the water we
    threw from our washbowl this morning that drowns him
Perhaps the friendly greeting we gave the stranger locked her
    in a madhouse for years – strangers fear kindness in our
    city
And its true that kids in the playing fields kick up the dust
    that blinds the last sight in old peoples' eyes

But the wheatfield is hungry ! – do not offer it one ear of
    wheat !
The storm is tormented ! – it beats its head on your roof – do
    not mop up one tear with your sleeve !
The fisherman's family must build their house on the sand:
    they live from the sea
But we have the care of the world
And we have built houses of sand on rock
And that we have not accepted that
Is the lie concerning self

Free

Imagine a stream that leaps from a high pass between
    granite mountains
And drives us before it
Our lives and possessions – our homes and streets and
    factories – our cities of towers and shopping arcades
The table at which we seat guests – our clothes – the sheets
    that flap on the lines – the stores of war and the tins in our
    cupboards
All driven before the stream to the front of the spate
And jut from it like a figurehead !

There are two ways to escape
By drowning
Or in the frenzy that sucks us back from the spate and spins
    us in whirlpools where garbage is stacked on towerblock
    stairs and fallen streetlamps block the carriageways and
    wind scatters the sawdust from the skin of one ragdoll into
    the skin of another

Otherwise we stay at the front of the flood – the point of the
    spate – thrust from the tide like a figurehead
The great weight of water fills us with the torrent's speed
We rush with the water that drives us before it
The power of history that weighs us with chains forces us to
    be free

Sonnets

Sonnets

1.

Simplicity that excludes complicates
Simplicity that includes is hard to achieve
The tallest tower rests on the earth
You dont say buried men have their feet on the ground
A seed falls as if dead
And comes to life when it lays at rest
The clock hands point away from each other
To tell the same time
Nailed to the wall the flag is clear
Carried in wind or draped on a catafalque
It is hard to read

2.

Animals lie – the weasel dances for the rabbit
The hare plays dead and the nightjar flutters
All lions are alike
The lion that is stronger is more like a lion
Only people deceive themselves
They are like cogs in a machine that think it moves so that
   they may turn
When it breaks down
To them it may seem to be working better
When they learn what it makes
To them it may seem to be playing tricks

3.
You have power and therefore you must dictate
Dictators' power destroys
The weak have no power and therefore they must dictate
What else can they do ?
It has always been so
If they say 'do this'
And you put aside your power and do it
Perhaps when they spoke you heard them say
'What manner of person are you ?'
A question that is not answered with soldiers and computers
No doubt a thing done freely is better done
But we dont often read of such things
In newspapers or history books
And done by dictators they are no more
Than lightning flashes that show us
The drenching rain
The starving have no alternative
They must take the dictator's power
So that all things are done freely and well
Or die
That is their power

4.
When science is used to make lies more elegant
So that teachers no longer flinch
At the questions in children's faces
When the bones of the starving are ground
And fed to the fields
So that the rich may reap richer harvests
When the sewer is bigger than the sea
In which it voids
When the graves are too small
For the bodies that wait beside them for burial
And at last lies no longer pass for truth
They will go to the oracle
But the oracle is the first thing they destroyed
So that they were free to destroy the rest

5.
Monstrous plants grow from seeds of truth
The enemy-humiliated little corporal
Was less destructive than his enemies: they created him
When half the world lay in their shadow
The monster grew in the dark
Twisting to reach the light
And called all jews exploiters – rich and poor
And the leather-and-silk thugs of the Prussian Staff harmless
    victims
Seeds that cannot grow in light
Twist in the dark
Like deadmen's fingers reaching for triggers

6.
The past has long been full of crimes so terrible
That no one can live at peace
Till the crimes have been told and put right
But the past is full of crimes so terrible
That no one can live at peace
Till the consequences are dealt with
But the past is full of crimes so terrible
That no one can live at peace
Till we have dealt with the last of the consequences
That is why history is just

7.
Again and again the world turns to darkness
Ten times in our lives murder has been as common
As walking the streets
The sky that should watch in peace over the city
Became a murderer's eye seeing all things
Religion and philosophy did not stand against the flood
That ate our walls with insatiable appetite
What are our daily lives ?
For money and power we threaten with knives and words
Our tongues twist like snakes sloughing their skin
Should it surprise us that when the killing starts
Some are chosen by name and others by chance or lot ?
We are like Judas who lives by selling his hanging

8.

Weapons on show-stands and in museum cases
Stone dirks struck before history
Crusaders' knuckle-dusters
The axes of teutonic knights
Cannons fired at ramillies
The first bombers of wire and wood
Missiles like deformed giants' foetuses
They are displayed but do not belong to the past
The army would raid the museums
If their new weapons were not better killers
In the long hours of watching
Between the fixed routines of maintenance
And the dummy countdowns
The watchers in well-laundered tunics
Swap comics
If the rockets are not put in museums
We will be displayed with dinosaurs' bones

9.

Wherever we look – wherever we go – there are ruins
Is anyone left to tell us why we died ?
We were told to be dead so we're dead
The body may live when the mind
Is dust under our feet or fingers
Or the ashes that bury others
We must discover why we died
Or our lives are like half-spelt names on a stone
Waiting for the chisel to finish them
We were so confused by the order
We forgot to ask what it meant
Before we obeyed it
But if we connect our death to the order
We'll know why we died
When we see the bread is cut
We know there's a knife: then its safe to eat
And when we know why we died
We shall live

10.

From time to time in human affairs
Facts give way to fiction
To do one thing we believe many things
And if for a time we believe fictions
The fact that we are humans
Gives way to the fiction we are monsters
And when we live in fiction we pay in fact
Later when we look at the stones and broken bones
We wonder how we ever believed such lies !
We are not evil
But because we desire that others be happy
We are cruel
If we believe fictions we sink in corruption
And the corruption of the living
Is worse than the corruption of the dead
Who only breathe into our nostrils
But cannot act

11.

Can your children play in the street ?
Your wife open your door without flinching ?
Can you look through your windows
And not peer into the undergrowth ?
Is only the night dark and nothing done in it
That cannot be done by day ?
In the morning can you say to your friends
We will meet in the evening ?
Yes if you kill the wolf at your door

12.

It is not permitted to enter the minister's office
The school staff-room the sanctuary or the banker's vault
Yet here the housewife passes on the shortcut to the shops
The young girl cycles to work – against local bylaws
The old man looks at the trees and stones hardly bigger than
    dolls' houses
And people come to bury their dead
In the council estate beyond the low wall
Washing flaps on the lines and the children shout
Here where the dead pay their great respect to the living
The earth is mostly sky
And the empty bread-wrapper is as beautiful as the flowers

13.

I woke in the night
Rain fell on the roof
From the sound I learned
That a wailing woman had stood at my door
And left while I slept
Five times that night she came
Each time I looked through the window
At the armies parading before the moon
I did not go down to let the storm into my house
And each time she went away
Who was the wailing woman who came to my door ?
In dreams and the places near them
We forget that some have died
And cannot open the door
But she does not come from the dead
Five times in the night
I sent her from the house
To see what I cannot see
Alive we are crude
We move and things run away
In the morning I go down and unfasten the lock
And day waits at the door

14.

Treat the world courteously
Regret each time we must shoulder aside a bush
How else shall we set the iron plough to the turf
Sail the laden barge through the canal
And drive before the wind ?
When you put ugliness in your face you corrupt light
Rancour – the voices of fools shouting orders to stones
Those who entrust their humanity to the gods lose it
Listen carefully to the child's questions
How else will you solve riddles in the laboratory ?
Be stronger than your rulers
And defend yourself against your enemies
That also is care of the world
And some wounds – when we cure them we die
But treat the world gently
Or our children will live under our graves

15.

All men and women are mortal
At last they are earth and water and fire and a little air
All things that live journey on one road
They may not stop or turn aside
And rest is only walking a little slower
No one returns
No love is strong enough to call a lover from death
Nor hate strong enough to drag back an enemy
But as we walk we may look at those beside us
And those ahead may turn to call to those who follow
And as we cannot change one step we have taken
We are content
And if the road were longer we would fall at the same place
And if we could turn back lose our strength at the same hour

16.

The constant stars set on their course
The sun that lights its way and never sees darkness
The moon that bears its journeys from emptiness to
    brightness
Crossed the sky before we lived on earth
Where grey clouds frown over the mouths of frightened seas
And our fierce passions make ruins black
Ancients called them gods but they were before the gods
We should be like them
And see all things yet not leave the course

17.

When rain darkened the marble slab
On which lay a heap of seeds
No more than a child could hold in its hand
They sprouted green fleshy tails
And when the rain stopped
The puddle that looked as deep as the sea
Dried in an hour
Birds scavenged the shoots and scattered the empty husks
And on the marble slab where the seeds had been
Left brown curly stains
Till wind and rain scoured them out too
But I still see them
As if their dust or dust from the street
Lay on the ends of my eyelashes

18.

On these hills armies fought battles
Bones lie where grass and birches tremble
The child holds my hand and asks why there is no war ?
I answer: no son is sent with an automatic rifle
To execute families on days he does not even write in his
     diary
And no one buys another's labour
Justice is simple
It cannot be sold in the market or bought in court
No one can appeal against its sentence
Each is his own gaoler
In time the murderers are arraigned
And the dead go to the stand to give their incorruptible
     evidence

19.

By what light shall you die ?
In a night screamed at by owls
Or a morning in the chatter of wards ?
Or to the engrossed voices of children at play ?
Will death watch you from your window for years
Or suddenly come round a corner
And throw a mortuary sheet in your eyes ?
Some you questioned have since died
They told you nothing
But it is certain
If you die in streets wailing the city's pain
You were dead this morning when you opened your windows

20.

There will not be a world
In which no voice rises in anger
And all desires bring joy
Great causes will stand in the balance
But bodies and souls will not be sold
To tradesmen whose business is not even known
The butcher goes to market and lies to the cattle
What use are lies to cattle?
It is better for them to name the trade and the trader
The buyers of people also lie
Each day the master tells new lies to his people
To cover the old lies that fall apart
What use are lies to such people?
For them truth has all the advantage of lies
It is better for them to name the trade and the trader
Their master has uses for lies
They are the only people who have
A use for freedom

21.

We are children of the sword and our fathers sold their
  brothers
But those who cut the furrow know the sword may till
Not all who cry peace peace can live without war
They kill the dove and read the entrails for battles
They make a brand of the olive branch and burn down the
  house
It is easier for corn to grind stone than stone to grind corn
That is why men go to war
But when there is peace stone will grind corn
Women will call their neighbours to sit at their table
The mad king will not weep while his fool jokes
And Cain will bear his mark like a scar
And know that rust on the sword does not heal the wound
Peace is won by those who can live with it
It is the struggle for reason
We called for peace and our rulers waged war on us
We won the victories that defeated us
But when we make war on our rulers
We will defeat war and give victory its peace

Work Poems

Work Poems

Human Cannon

The Unnamed Child

She would not name her child
What use was a name ?
She could never call its name as it played in the street and it
    could never answer
Unknown soldiers have graves
In concentration camps there are ash-heaps of nameless
Those who lie together in mass graves in europe and asia did
    not know each other's name
And who can name the dust of Hiroshima ?
Whole cities are named after their graveyards

Human Cannon didnt live in a human world – she lived in
     our world
Her child didnt feel her breast
To her it was blasphemy to name a child in an inhuman
     world
Cruelty to behave like a human mother in a world too
     inhuman to let her child live
Motherhood wounded her but the wound did not heal at birth
Death renewed her birthpangs as many times as there are
     children's heads in the streets
Human Cannon's world had not yet been made human
It might have been named after her child's death !
But when she had helped in the long work of making the
     world human
She named a village
And when that work is ended all children will bear her
     child's name

Monserrat

Mountain of teeth !
They say this was the shrine of the holy grail
The country lies like a giant on its back
Gnashing at the sky with its teeth – ripping – tearing it down
     to the ground !
Through a gap in the clouds light falls on the rows of teeth
     and Monserrat grins like the earth's mouth
In the storm lightning jumps over the teeth and Monserrat
     laughs
Chroniclers tell how in the war a mother knelt to support her
     son – then shook her fists at the sky
When she opened her hands – on each palm blood in the
     shape of a rose
She left the mountain and showed her hands to the people
They armed themselves against fascism
Yes it is only a legend !
But when the people arm themselves and bare their teeth
     Spain is a black dog menacing the sky with its fangs !

The War Plays

The Walking Woman

Think of it !
Walking seventeen years clutching her bundle and asking
    why ?
And when she was as dead as the land she trod she took new
    life as a dry bush twists in fire or a stone worn down by
    water takes on the sharpness of dragons' teeth
Her hair was a wirebrush for scraping out engines – her eyes
    peered from under it as if a night-creature had gone to
    ground in her head
Her small plump feet took short steps in the rhythms of little
    scurries of rubble dislodging in ruins
Her hands were old and unskilled except in the craft of time –
    they grabbed or the fingers stuck out defensive
She wore a scarf against the wind

The world was grey with ash and the dust of cinders
At night and in storms – great darkness
Sometimes the clouds thinned till the sky was threadbare –
    then the light was bright
She said the military are mice – their droppings are
    everywhere – you can tell the places they have infected
She said teach children to avoid soldiers' shit

Nothing could happen to her that needed a response she had
    not already given
She experienced all she had to experience
She drained the cup – she tugged the tether to the end
She was more stone than stone and water than water

Years passed between her few meetings with others
One woman told her that child's a bundle – you feed it but
    the gruel stays in the bowl of the spoon
She answered what the child leaves I eat to teach it thrift
The woman said you eat to empty the spoon
She agreed and the woman left
Then she fed the bundle and said I told her you were rags to
    get rid of her

When the bundle spoke she grinned for days like a classroom
    of children
The rags would explain the mystery of the world
When it fell silent she wept and raged
Was it sickening ? Sulking ? Dead ? How could she tell when
    the signs of life were so little ?
She straightened the rags and went on

She was not yet empty and had not yet experienced all things
    that were in her to experience when a young woman who
    had taught her not to kill questioned her
She answered what do you want with an old woman with
    hands like the skulls of birds on withered sticks ?
In saying this she mourned for her life which must be held
    against her – but she had not yet experienced all things
    that were in her to experience
The young woman said: then turn away
She gave as answer: although she would not go with the
    young woman the young woman would be her friend

When she was old she met her son
He sat on the ground with his face bowed on his bent knees
    and his hands clutched over his crossed ankles
She embraced him and held out the bundle
He stood and held out his hands to take it
He said come with me to the settlement – you're needed –
    much to do – work – teach
She would not

For seventeen years she asked why ? why ? why ? and found
    no answer
Now when her son befriended her she asked him the question
    and he gave her a coat from the settlement store
A coat – for her !
She wheezed and pointed – a coat !
Once she'd've grabbed it and run
Now she pointed a finger as long as a thigh-bone and
    doubled over with soundless laughter – a coat !
For the woman who'd eaten the fruit that grows on the
    burned bush !

When all she had left was the bundle she gave it away
And when she was empty and had experienced all things
    that were in her to be experienced
When the world was dust yet she could have found in it one
    grain she sought and told each grain from the others
(For in us there is much that we may experience)
She hoisted the roads she had walked onto her back as if they
    were a bundle of sticks
And went on

After the Raid

For a while I stopped running and trying to find direction
I stood by the street and watched others pass
Many carried small bundles like birds with debris in their
    beaks seeking a tree for their nest in a burned forest
Children had lost their parents and parents had lost each
    other
The old stumbled with the weariness of blind infants
Carts creaked by – their wheels were large so that one beast
    could draw them in rough country
Now people drew them in ruins
They were piled with the dead
I asked what liquid ran from under the carts
The bodies on top pressed it from the bodies below

It was the chyle of the dead
The city was silent except where the buried moaned so that
    it seemed the ruins sang to themselves
Black smoke unfolded in the sky
On the broken walls huge shadows glided and leaped among
    those who went by as if the living were being taken
    prisoner by the dead
Already in the past there were signs
The merchants built high towers but where money came
    from even the bankers didnt know
It was as if the heavy ledgers squeezed it from the rows of
    figures
Twelve years ago I came to this city
On one side of the road a line of carts with big wheels
Each with a farmer hunched over his whip facing the mule
His family behind him facing backwards
All silent after the day's work
On the other side of the road a long line of automobiles
With drivers in coney-island shirts and passengers bent over
    maps
Even then the river and port had been deserted
One or two pleasure boats
In a few years people started to flee from the soldiers: each
    soldier was an ant colony shut up in steel
And birth was labour chore beside the coffin
I started to walk again
When the tall towers had reared up and thrown the earth
    like a blanket over their shaking shoulders
Fire had burned off the leaves and blackened the bark of an
    apple tree
But the burnt fruit still hung on the boughs
No road led from ruins
The skeletons inside people chose the way the people went
    and those who wished to go another way fought with their
    own skeleton
Or perhaps the skeletons were trying to flee from such
    pitiless flesh
It was the end of time

Dead Soldiers

I

Often its hard to believe people have done what they've done
  – yet the reports are accurate
The mind has contrived reasons for whatever the body may
  do
Or will contrive them in certain circumstances
To understand anyone's action – human or inhuman – we
  have only to describe it precisely

II

The dead get on with the business of living
Eat – sleep – tie up their rags – breathe
Contradiction is a sign of life
The dead acknowledge stages of dying – sometimes they lie
  still and rot or fall behind and are lost
Many dead die again as if the body's weight squeezed out
  the last shreds of life

III

From the hillside we saw the mist in the valley – a stranded
  sea creature
It came slowly but to us it seemed rapid as if speeded up by
  a projector
When it was close we saw the edges were blurred
It fell on us – licking our faces – inside our cuffs and collars –
  the tongues seemed to be in us – the body eating the inside
  of its own skin – the muscles sucking the bones – exactly
  like that
It passed and rolled up the hill – things sticking out –
  furniture – clothes – radios – a goalposts
Like gravel stuck on a snowball
We were silent for half an hour
We heard the drops of mist running down the stems of grass
Then we understood we were dead

IV
Sometimes the dead hold a formal discussion
When you're alive you know you're alive and now we know
　we're dead
Prove it with a rope round the neck ? One of us starve ?
He'd rot and vanish but he'd still see us and know we're
　dead
Vanishing ? Rotting ? How does that prove you're alive or
　dead ?

Great Peace

Yesterday she died
Slowly towards evening she saw she must die
Like all those who reach her age she had died several times
    without learning much from death
The dead were dolls – discarded pieces of plaster bound in
    the wire that had once set them free
She left part of her mind as you might leave a room to others
    to live in but still listen to the voices that sound through
    the walls like the creaking of trees beyond hedges
She spoke of hope – now she's dead she knows its not needed
A few days of confusion and funeral fuss till the dead flowers
    are thrown away and the undertaker is paid
The dead are freed from time but patient with the living
Their death has put them in great danger
If they see legs in a ditch they climb in and pull the man
    from under the gun carriage
They take down the wounded's groans in a script that is read
    back as words
Their gestures seem to fight with the wind and tug at its hair
Do not watch for them – they are not themselves and have
    not become someone else
No nirvanas heavens or toys
In winter when bonfires were lit in the kent orchards black
    shapes tended the glowing braziers and white smoke
    drifted under the frosty trees
The sloes rotted and dripped
But out in the lanes the hedgerow apples ripened as if a
    mouth breathed in the ice and the ice protects the breath
    that melts it
And there is a pale red glow in the frost on the fruit

A Sheath of Poems

My boy enquired 'What is the meaning of "enemy" ?'
Kazan replied 'My son, the meaning of "enemy"
is the people whom we kill when we catch them
and when they catch us they kill us'.

The Book of Dede Korkut translated by
Geoffrey Lewis

A Sheath of Poems

Strange Fruit

There is a tree with dark foliage
The fruit that grow on it are human hands
They do not ripen in the sun
Autumn passes and leaves them as white as snow
And one night under orders
They pick up the saw and axe and tackle
And cut down the tree on which they grow

Mildenhall

Three hundred thousand visitors come from the cities to the
   air display
Crews guide families through bombers
Youth clubs are lectured by officers at control panels – the
   dim x-rayed bones of fingers on lighted buttons
Elderly ladies clutching rolled plastic macs peer down the
   hatches of low security silos
Hotdogs – fried onions – canned music
The Great Fly Over !
Fathers hold their daughters' hands and point to dots on the
   horizon
Sons bounce on their mother's shoulders
Flapping hair – programmes blowing away
Three hundred thousand faces stare at the sky – then turn as
   one – jets scream – the shadows pass over the white face of
   a giant doll
No bombs
Later when the visitors go the traffic jams cant spoil the
   day's outing – 'see you next year' – 'it makes you proud of
   your country'
In the evening quiet a few figures hunched in grey plastic
   suits and rubber boots move like robots about the runways
The airmen who later will kill the spectators
   Who dont even force the hangmen to build a gallows in
   their street
   But let themselves be hanged from the lintels of their front
   doors

Flowers are Always Welcome

A tired porter sat to rest for a moment on the stone steps of a
  bank
His shadow sat there long after the currency had crashed
A sentry turned to go off duty
His shadow kept watch long after the war had been lost
Passers-by in the street
Their shadows burned on bricks hurried to destinations that
  had long ago vanished in fire
Even the patterns on dresses were branded into their
  wearer's skin
On one woman's shoulders the shapes of lilacs
It could be said the airmen had sent flowers to her funeral

Cenotaph

Around the political brass and army brass and commercial
  brass and confectionary royals
Service rows of men and women as stiff as pork on hooks in a
  cold store
The National Head comes forward to place a wreath on the
  tall grave beneath which no one is buried
And bends once in the middle
At roughly the place a soldier grasps when a bullet enters his
  belly
And there should be a day when the National Head did not
  reach the empty grave
But fell (in mime) with the wreath on top
So that for once a soldier's death is acted out on the day of
  remembrance
Till such things are seen all soldiers living and dead are
  unknown

The Shabby Suit

In the newspapers
Cenotaph Sensation – Leader of Loyal Opposition Shabbily
   Dressed – Unfit for Ceremony – Pained Eyes Averted !
A crowd of skeletons in pierced helmets and rotting rags
   smelling of trench rat-water
Awkwardly hanging about
Saw him and said
One of us in this crew of gangsters !
And ran to stand at his side and would have shaken his hand
   if their bones had not been as thin as air
The Brass People and Jewel Family did not see them
They were busy admiring their own uniforms
Which are the gold braid and epaulettes on scarecrows' rags

Silence

Each year two minutes' silence before the fallen millions
Perhaps if we stood in silence before those yet to fall
The father's silence before his child might last three minutes
The woman's silence before her lover might last a week
And the silence of strangers before each other might stretch
   to a month
So that as we stared at those who had not yet fallen our daily
   tumult would stop
And a great silence spread
And later when we went about our business perhaps we
   would deal justly with one another
So that the long chain of distortions – the orders – the threats
   and cajolings – the wages and medals – would end and the
   price of freedom no longer be death ?
Without justice there is always war
It is decreed in the infant's stammer and inscribed in the
   atom even when it's split
When we live in justice we will not need to be silent before
   the fallen
They will not fall

No

All slaves – all martyrs of swords and stakes – all massacred
    and murdered – all dead soldiers and civilian war-dead
All who suffered the last agony of the wall or rope
Who felt the last anger – who shouted the last accusation
Who were made stronger by the last confirmation or stunned
    by the last sudden insight
Who in the last moment mourned more deeply for the dead
    about them than you can mourn with all your banners and
    bands
If they lived their shout of *no* would silence your war signals
And their marches block the roads to your silos and bunkers
That is how they would save you – those who you say died to
    save you
But you have only the living to reason with you and show
    you what you will suffer !
How greatly the dead must mourn for the living and weep
    over their cities !

Sports Ground Inferno

Ranks of spectators in the wooden stand
Excitement ! Sensation ! – the match swings this way and
   that
Sudden heat – spectators look round – they watch the clothes
   of others near them smoulder and burst into flames
The floor crackles – in an instant the roof is a rolling sea of
   fire
Those who escape to the pitch look back
In the bright furnace they see dark blemishes like lumps of
   coal – bodies
A man in blazing clothes and with an expressionless face
   comes from the flames
And strolls – that is the word witnesses will use later – over
   the pitch
Others sit upright in their seats as flames run between them
   along the handrails
They do not seem to know what is happening to them or
   what they might do to save themselves
Later that day survivors will stand by the charred corpses
   and tell how they had felt they were in a dream
And in this way one saturday afternoon as women worked or
   drank tea with their neighbours and children played or fed
   their pets
The little holocaust fell on the busy city where many
   dreamed and did not know what they might do to save
   themselves

Inheritance

So many ruins ! Such desolation !
All this destruction your parents created so that you might
    be free !
They wrecked the world for the sake of your future !
All this wilderness you inherit from their hands !
For them no trouble was too great ! No pains were spared on
    your behalf !
    Be thankful ! – the wind howled as it swept over the
        children's graves

Victory

Victory !
How shall we tell the good news ?
Shout it in the ears of the dead and hope the surprise will
    wake them ?
Yell it in the ruins so the echo passes it on ?
Tap it out on the bones – a glimmering might get through to
    the skull ?
Write it on labels tied to dead infants' wrists – when their
    mothers find them they can rejoice at the good news !
Or scrawl it on the dust ? – if the fire storms dont pass this
    way perhaps people from another world might read it !
Dont concern yourself with the problem
You wont live to face it

Prepare for Peace

The ancients said let all who would live in peace prepare for
  war
We prepared for war
We waged it
Where is the peace ?

Armies march and the ground trembles !
When the olive branch is offered you count the leaves !
A child screams – you ask whose child !
To save your child you massacre the innocents – it's not
  human !
Prepare for peace !
That is the gift for all children !

When you burn your neighbour's house the fire will spread
  to your house !
War is a mouth that shouts slogans and eats its own head !
We prepared for war !
Where is the peace ?
Prepare for peace !
That is the gift to all children !

I Am Tired of the Human Spirit

After the nights bright with fire and the days dark with
    smoke
Things get back to normal
Before long weeds grow in the ruins
Friendly bars welcome the conquerors
And in the souvenir kiosks traders sell pieces of twisted glass
It is a kindness to shuffle the maimed out of sight
And the other survivors are reassured when the official
    enquiry hides the causes of death under a great cloud of
    secrets
The human spirit cannot be defeated any more than walls of
    air can hold back a flood
And so Hiroshima prospers
I wish it didnt
Not that I want the suffering to continue
But to say you cannot go on suffering
In time scars wear out the skin they heal
Bones break under the weight of splints
And throats choke on hymns of thanksgiving
When you suffer do not be brave
Wail like a siren in the streets
And when your rulers make weapons to defend the city made
    from the ruins weapons made
Get rid of your rulers: they are your enemy !

SDP

I said to the politician
With a blow torch burn out the plastic doll's eyes
Open its stomach with a chisel and poke your fingers
    through the hole so that we may see how the entrails will
    fall

The politician said
Such talk disturbs the people
I am the wise ruler
The gentle guide
I seek the middle way

Perhaps the people should be disturbed ?
Surely they will be greatly put out when the fire falls on their
    heads ?
And shouldnt the citizens know how the city will be
    defended ?

We should say to the wise leader who seeks the middle way
On that day when you approach the mother in the street she
    will fling her child's entrails in your face

Ode

It is easy to say ban the bomb
Will you change your society ?
Will you replace the owners with the owned ?
Your quiet ease – your sensitive soul – your cultured taste –
    the pangs of your conscience – the cleanliness under your
    nails – all these are protected by the injustice of classes
Great violence is needed to defend your way of life
Great rage to swim in the sea of shipwrecks
Minds must be numbed with ignorance – emotions made
    rabid with cunning and craft
That is the workshop where bombs are made !
Always where there is injustice there is war
All who live in injustice make war – shout peace and mean
    bombs !
They build bridges of water ! Shelters of sighs to keep out the
    hurricane !
They say ban the bomb but to save the world they would not
    alter the hour at which they sat down to their tea-table

Why Bombs Are Made

In the past storms and plagues fell on the people
Kings dont know the laws of community
And philosophers hadnt written the books of change
Priests said that suffering came from the gods
But gods dont make bombs

Rulers – owners – all who have privilege
Teach that in democracy all share one freedom so all must
    share its defence
But if all is to be shared when will the rich share their
    wealth ? The owners their factories and newspapers ? The
    privileged their hospitals and schools ?
The poor still pay the rich
The weak bear the strong
The innocent suffer the punishment of the guilty
The owner robs those he hires yet he is the judge and
    lawmaker – the priest and teacher
And so he orders the meaning of things
That is why his democracy is a tyranny of lies !
It is not the problem that confounds us but the solution
It is not the exploitation that makes us poor but the prizes
It is not the crime that destroys but the rewards
It is not the conviction that condemns us but the pardon
It is not the cell the imprisons us but the open door
The blunt instrument wounds us – the law cripples us
Do not flinch from the handcuffs and blows in the face but
    from the pat on the back
Do not shudder at the abuse but at the praise
Do not dread the blackmailer but those who run with the
    ransom
Let the starving die if they must swallow lies with their
    bread !
Their children will choke on the lies – the violence and waste
    will not end for generations !
Those who believe lies become liars

In the confusion and chaos of your world who can believe the
    words in his own mouth or understand what his hand
    writes or tell where his feet take him ?
In your world fear must flourish and panic riot and people
    run with the mad
And that is why bombs are made

Your society must make bombs and you belong to it
The healthy stomach feeds the sick brain – the sound limbs
    carry the diseased heart – and the simple acts of your daily
    life make bombs
When you wrap your children's lunch you open the plans
When you buy your newspaper you order the raw materials
When you cheer the jewel-élite you go to work in the
    ordnance factory
When you shop in the supermarket you choose the targets
When you watch TV you sit at control panels
You turn your living-room into the yard where looters are
    shot
Your kitchen reeks of disposal pits
Your bedsheets cover the dead on runways
And in your arsenals the guns aimed at distant targets point
    at your head
Do not pray to the gods – you make the bombs that destroy
    you

You say ban the bomb
The cog tells the machine to make something new
The machine will make what it always makes
To make something new you must change the machine
Change it ! – or when you shout ban the bomb you make
    bombs
Change your society ! – and the struggle for justice will make
    your life human

You

If lying outside your door you found a stranger scarred and
    scantly clad in rags
Flesh showed through the holes like faces staring from ruins
And blind
And the mouth an empty plate on which the teeth lay aslant
    like nibbled bones –
I tell you these things for a reason –
And the fluid that ran from the ears was as dark as oil from a
    sump
Perhaps you would stoop and gathering this person into your
    arms go back into your house
Though you might turn away in despair or rage or even
    disgust
Now you are this stranger
And bear the marks of the neglect you show yourself
When you let your rulers turn your city into a butcher's
    block

There Is No Precedent

In the past soldiers died for civilians
Now civilians die for soldiers
Homes are gunposts guarding barracks
The town square is a tank trap
Schools are trenches in front of government bunkers
Peace ? – the time when people arm their enemies and train
    to be killed
Politicians hold children and unarmed people – millions and
    millions – hostage
There is no precedent !
Rivers wont hold the blood they'll spill
The sky wont have space for the smoke from their fires
The deserts will be too small for the dust of their ruins
Preparing such devastation can't be called government
There is no precedent !
Patriotism ? – the training of murderers
Respecting tradition ? – fawning on media idols
Education ? – the barking of barbarians
Culture ? – the tattooing of corpses
Religion ? – the devil's creed in the mouths of gods
Defence ? – cattle herding people to abattoirs
Progress ? – the dead digging their graves
No nation can survive such corruption
In the past the people longed to be free of their sufferings
We have the power to be free and use it to make a prison

In War

In war they will suffer – your husband and wife – your
    parents and children – your neighbours and friends
All who live in your town or village – your country or
    overseas
They will perish as surely as if you ran from one to the other
    and put a bullet into each head
And from house to house and threw a petrol bomb in the
    window

Later officers will feed the dead to computers and the
    computers will break them down
Rulers will unveil plaques on bunker walls to honour those
    who died for the freedom of bunkers – then poke round for
    a new generation
And priests will bless the plaques and the dead and the new-
    born

You earn your slavery well ! – you who let those who rule in
    your name do things you'd cut off your hand before you'd
    lift it to do yourself !
And for this you will howl in ruins and wander in charred
    fields
Stumble over your neighbours' bones
And crawl to your grave over the graves of your fathers and
    mothers and it will be filled with your children's ashes !
Is this how you will end your days ?
For the slave there is only one salvation – one freedom –
    know you are a slave

If Stones Could Speak

The earth will not speak
It will be harder than iron
Stones will not weep
Wind will scorch even the moisture the first volcanoes left
    deep in granite
The roar of the fire will drown the calls of those in the fire
There will be a wilderness but no beast to howl out the
    world's misery
But on that day when the dust is silent
The stones will say:
Now they will weep ! – so great is the suffering that even
    human beings will cry out against it